Ranger Rick's NatureScope

WILD ABOUT WEATHER

National Wildlife Federation

LEARNING TRIANGLE PRESS

*Connecting
kids, parents, and teachers
through learning*

An imprint of McGraw-Hill

New York San Francisco Washington, D.C. Auckland Bogotá Caracas
Lisbon London Madrid Mexico City Milan Montreal New Delhi
San Juan Singapore Sydney Tokyo Toronto

Library of Congress Cataloging-in-Publication Data applied for

McGraw-Hill
A Division of The McGraw-Hill Companies

NATIONAL WILDLIFE FEDERATION®

1 2 3 4 5 6 7 8 9 JDL/JDL 9 0 2 1 0 9 8 7

ISBN 0-07-047098-7

NatureScope® was originally conceived by National Wildlife Federation's School Programs Editorial Staff, under the direction of Judy Braus, Editor. Special thanks to all of the Editorial Staff, Scientific, Educational Consultants and Contributors who brought this series of eighteen publications to life.

NATIONAL WILDLIFE FEDERATION EDITORIAL STAFF
Creative Services Manager: Sharon Schiliro
Editor, Ranger Rick® magazine: Gerry Bishop
Director, Classroom-related Programs: Margaret Tunstall
Contributors: Tornadoes! by Greg Stumpf; Forecasting the Weather, Follow the Weather, What Was the Weather Like?, Running a Weather Radar, and A Vote for Forecasting by Dr. William Gallus; updated Copycat activities by Thomas Richard Baker from his book *Weather in the Lab* (McGraw-Hill, 1993); The Man Who Named the Clouds by Stephen Kramer; and Depending on the Weather by Hamline University

McGRAW-HILL EDP STAFF
Acquisitions Editor: Judith Terrill-Breuer
Editorial Supervisor: Patricia V. Amoroso
Production Supervisor: Claire Stanley
Designer: York Production Services
Cover Design: David Saylor

OTHER TITLES IN *RANGER RICK'S NATURESCOPE*

GOAL

Ranger Rick's NatureScope is a creative education series dedicated to inspiring in children an understanding and appreciation of the natural world while developing the skills they will need to make responsible decisions about the environment.

A CLOSE-UP LOOK AT
WILD ABOUT WEATHER

L ooking at the Table of Contents, you can see we've divided *Wild About Weather* into five chapters (each of which deals with a broad weather theme), a craft section, and an appendix. Each of the five chapters includes *background information* that explains concepts and vocabulary, *activities* that relate to the chapter theme, and *Copycat Pages* that reinforce many of the concepts introduced in the activities.

You can choose single activity ideas or teach each chapter as a unit. Either way, each activity stands by itself and includes teaching objectives, a list of materials needed, suggested age groups, subjects covered, and a step-by-step explanation of how to do the activity. (The objectives, materials, age groups, and subjects are highlighted in the left-hand margin for easy reference.)

AGE GROUPS

The suggested age groups are:

- Primary (grades K–2)
- Intermediate (grades 3–5)
- Advanced (grades 6–8)

Each chapter begins with primary activities and ends with intermediate or advanced activities. But don't feel bound by the grade levels we suggest. You'll be able to adapt many of the activities to fit your particular age group and needs.

OUTDOOR ACTIVITIES

There's no better way to study weather than to go outside. So we've tried to include at least one outdoor activity in each chapter. These are coded in the chapters in which they appear with this symbol:

COPYCAT PAGES

The *Copycat Pages* supplement the activities and include ready-to-copy games, puzzles, coloring pages, worksheets, and mazes. *Answers to all Copycat Pages are on the inside back cover or in the texts of the activities.*

WHAT'S AT THE END

The sixth section, *Crafty Corner,* will give you some art and craft ideas that complement many of the activities in the first five chapters. And the last section, the *Appendix,* is loaded with reference suggestions that include books, films, and weather supplies. The Appendix also has weather questions and answers, a weather glossary, and suggestions for where to go for more weather information.

FITTING IT ALL IN

We've tried to combine the science activities in *Wild About Weather* with language arts, history, creative writing, geography, math, social studies, and art activities to make this booklet as versatile as possible. If you plan to do an entire unit on weather, *Wild About Weather* can be your major source of background information and activity ideas. But if you have time to use only a few of the activity ideas, check the objectives and subjects to see which ones will complement what you're already doing.

We hope *Wild About Weather* will provide you with a source of activity ideas and project suggestions that you can use over and over again with your groups.

WHAT'S "NORMAL" WEATHER?

If you live in Fort Worth, Texas, your "normal" weather is going to be a lot different from what's normal for Boston, Massachusetts. The Pacific Ocean, the Gulf of Mexico, the Atlantic Ocean, the Rocky Mountains, the Adirondack Mountains, and many other bodies of water and landforms influence local weather in different parts of the United States and Canada.

In *Wild About Weather* we have tried to explain general weather concepts and patterns, realizing that specific weather patterns will vary greatly from one area to another. We suggest that before you teach a weather unit or conduct a weather program, you talk to a meteorologist in your area to find out what's special about your weather, how it changes from season to season, and how it might be different from typical weather patterns.

TABLE OF CONTENTS

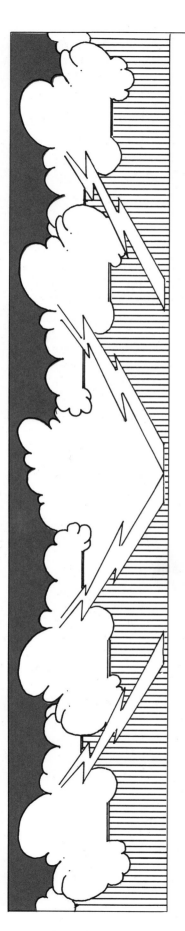

WHAT MAKES THE WEATHER?

It's raining on tadpoles in Paris
And snowing on deer in Peru.
There's hail falling down in Montana
And it's clobbered a cricket or two.

The fish in Dakota are freezing,
The rabbits in Florida "sweat."
It's drizzling on horses in Scotland,
And leopards are wet in Tibet.

High winds in the Canadian Rockies
Are keeping the sheep on the run.
What makes all this crazy old weather?
Just the earth, water, air, and the sun!

That's right. These four "ingredients"—the sun, the earth, air, and water—shape all the weather we know. What is weather? It's the condition of the atmosphere—from tornadoes ripping across a valley to the fluffy white clouds you see drifting in the sky on a summer day. Here's how these four weather makers work together to create our weather:

AIR

The earth is surrounded by a huge ocean of air that stretches from the earth's surface to the beginning of outer space. This ocean of air is called the atmosphere. Without it, we wouldn't have to worry about the weather. It wouldn't exist and neither would we!

We're All Airheads: Every time you take a breath of air, you are taking in a very special mixture of gases and aerosals (tiny droplets and particles). The most common ingredients of air are the gases nitrogen and oxygen. But carbon dioxide; water vapor; bits of smoke, dust, and pollen; and tiny, tiny droplets of water and ice crystals can also be in the air.

Let's Hear It for the Atmosphere: The atmosphere is life's security blanket. It absorbs harmful radiation from the sun and burns up meteors before they hit the earth. It also lets just enough of the sun's rays through to warm the earth during the day without frying us, and at night it holds in enough of this heat to keep us from freezing. Without the atmosphere, temperatures could climb to over 200° F (93° C) during the day. At night they would quickly drop to more than 280° F (173° C) *below* zero. (That's what happens on the moon, where there is no atmosphere.)

The Layered Look: The atmosphere is one big ocean of air. But you can think of it as being divided into layers stacked one on top of the other. The lowest layer—the troposphere—is the one we live in and breathe. The troposphere is the only layer that has enough water vapor in it to form clouds or fog. That's one reason why almost all weather we see occurs in the troposphere.

Other layers of the atmosphere are the stratosphere, the mesosphere, the thermosphere, and the exosphere.

I Can't Take the Pressure: You might not think of air as having any weight, but it does. In fact, about a ton (0.9 t) of air pushes against each of us all the time, even though we can't really feel it. *Air pressure* is caused by the weight of this overlying air.

With all this pressure pushing against us, why aren't we crushed? It's because pressure inside our bodies equals the pressure from the atmosphere. People, like all other land animals, are especially adapted to living at this pressure.

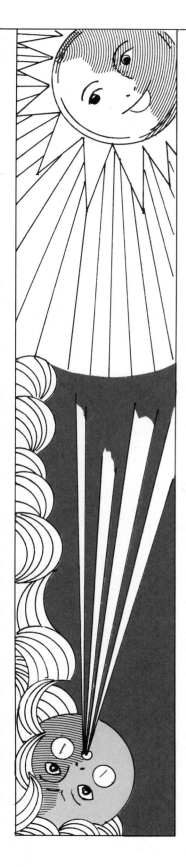

The Highs and Lows of Pressure: Air pressure is not exactly the same everywhere. One reason is that the temperature varies from place to place.

When air heats up, the air molecules move faster and faster. They push each other away, causing the air to expand. As the air expands, the molecules become more and more spread out and there are fewer molecules in the same amount of space. So the air in that space weighs less than it did when it was cooler and *exerts less pressure* on the earth. Cold air molecules are packed closer together, so cold air weighs more and *exerts more pressure* on the earth.

THE SUN

The sun cranks out radiation steadily. This radiation zips through space in all directions, traveling in the form of energy waves. Some of these waves we see as light (visible waves), some we feel as heat (infrared waves), and some we can neither see nor feel (X-rays, ultraviolet, TV, and radio waves).

Only about one two-billionth of the sun's energy even makes it to the earth's atmosphere. But this creates enough heat to stir up the atmosphere and make weather happen.

Soaking Up the Rays: Three things can happen when this solar radiation hits the earth's atmosphere:

- Some of the energy waves are absorbed by the atmosphere before they even get a chance to reach the earth.
- Some of the energy waves are reflected right back into space and don't heat up the earth at all. Clouds, snow, and volcanic ash are all energy *reflectors.*
- About half of the solar energy reaches the earth. This energy soaks into the earth's surfaces (land and water) and most is then re-radiated back into the air as heat waves.

Different surfaces absorb different amounts of sunlight and store different amounts of heat. For example, forests are dark and can absorb over 90% of the sunlight that reaches them. Oceans and other bodies of water can absorb anywhere from 60 to 96% of the sunlight that falls on them. But snow reflects most of the light and absorbs only about 25% or less.

THE EARTH

If the earth didn't revolve around the sun and spin on a tilted axis, the world's weather would be a lot different. For one thing, we wouldn't have seasons. And for another, the wind circulation around the globe would be much less complicated! (For more about winds, see the background information on pages 15–17.)

The Reasons for the Seasons: As the earth travels around the sun every year, different parts of the earth get more direct sunlight than others. When the North Pole is tilted toward the sun, the Northern Hemisphere has spring and summer.

(continued on next page)

During this time the Northern Hemisphere gets more direct sunlight and the days are longer than they are during fall and winter. (The same thing happens in the Southern Hemisphere when the South Pole is tilted toward the sun.)

Because the earth is spherical, areas near the equator get a lot of direct sunlight through the year. And areas near the poles don't get a lot of direct sun. (All places on the earth receive the same number of hours of sunlight each year. But the big difference is in the intensity of the sunlight that strikes the earth.) This unequal heating causes big differences in temperature and air pressure all over the earth.

WATER

You can't always see it, but water is in the air all the time. Sometimes the water in the air is in the form of a gas (water vapor), sometimes it's a liquid (tiny water droplets and larger raindrops), and sometimes it's a solid (ice crystals or snowflakes).

Sticky and Wet: If you live in an area that gets tropical air (air that is warm and humid) in summer, you can often feel water vapor in the air. It makes you feel "sticky," and the more water vapor in the air, the stickier you feel. The amount of water vapor in the air is called the *humidity*.

Hot Holds More: Humidity depends on the temperature of the air. Warm air can hold a lot more water vapor than cold air can. For example, if the temperature is 86° F (30° C), a cubic foot of air can hold one ounce (28 g) of water. But if the temperature is only 68° F (20° C), the same volume of air can hold only six-tenths of an ounce (17 g) of water. The *relative humidity,* which is the humidity reading given on the weather report, is the amount of vapor the air *is holding* expressed as a percentage of the amount the air *could hold* at that temperature. (The higher the relative humidity and the higher the temperature, the more water vapor in the air.)

Water on the Move: Heat evaporates millions of tons of water every day from lakes, streams, oceans, plants, and other sources. The liquid water changes to water vapor and mixes with the air. As the air is warmed by the sun, it rises. And as this moist, warm air rises higher, it expands and cools. It eventually cools so much that it can no longer hold all the water vapor it could when it was warm. So some water vapor *condenses* (changes to a liquid), forming clouds made up of tiny water droplets.

Under certain conditions, the water droplets in clouds can grow larger, freeze, or stick together (coalesce) and form precipitation (rain, snow, sleet, or hail). For more about precipitation, see the background information on pages 26–28.

Evaporation, condensation, and precipitation go on every minute of the day—and water recycles itself over and over again. For example, a molecule of water you drink today may have been part of a rain shower falling on Christopher Columbus or part of the Nile River when the pyramids were being built.

The sun is the source of energy that drives our weather. When this energy reaches the earth, it warms the earth's surfaces. But it warms the surfaces unevenly, with some areas getting more heat than others. This uneven heating moves the air (moving air is wind) and makes the water cycle work. And with the winds and water comes all our weather.

The Weather Master Myth

Write a weather myth after listening to one.

Objectives:
Describe how the earth, the sun, water, and air affect weather. Practice creative writing skills.

Ages:
Primary and Intermediate

Materials:
- *weather reference books*
- *paper and pencils*
- *magazines*
- *newspapers*
- *large pieces of cardboard*
- *glue*
- *markers*

Subjects:
Science, Creative Writing, and Arts and Crafts

Writing weather myths is one way children can learn more about weather while practicing their writing skills. First read "The Weather Master" to your group. It is a myth that explains in simple terms how the earth, the sun, air, and water all work together to create our weather. (You might also want to read some other myths, fables, or stories to the group about different subjects. For some classics, check *Aesop's Fables* or Rudyard Kipling's *Just So Stories*.)

Afterward, have your group create their own weather myths using the ideas we've listed on page 8 or using ideas they create themselves.

THE WEATHER MASTER

Once upon a time, in the days when the Universe was younger, the four weather makers—the Earth, the Sun, the Air, and the Water—decided to hold a huge weather celebration. So the Sun and the Air volunteered to send out the invitations to all the inhabitants of the world. And the Water and the Earth volunteered to find the best spot for the celebration.

But when the Earth saw the finished invitations, he wasn't very happy.

"They listed me last," the Earth said angrily. "Last! Why, I should be first. For without me there would be no weather at all!"

The Earth kept thinking as he spun around, "This just isn't right. I should be the Master of Weather. And the Sun, the Water, and the Air should take orders from me."

So the Earth sent out a notice to all the inhabitants of the world that said:

On the day of the celebration, we will hold a debate and elect the true Master of Weather. It is time someone took charge!

Well, the Sun and the Water and the Air were shocked. "What does he think he's doing?" exclaimed the Sun. "Without me there would be no heat. And without heat there would be no weather."

The Water was so mad she was steaming. "I am as important as the Earth. How dare he think he's more important!"

And the Air was so upset he just blew around muttering.

"I've got an idea, my friends," said the Sun. And she whispered to the other two weather makers. "We'll show the inhabitants of the world who's the most important."

On the day of the big celebration, all the inhabitants of the world came dressed in their best. The mountain wore his best snowy white coat. The sand came polished and gleaming. The lions and tigers and monkeys and camels were sleek and smooth. The butterflies and birds were clothed in bright colors. The oaks and maples were in their fall splendor. And even the mushrooms popped up fresh and new for the party.

"What a wonderful day for a celebration," said the trees and flowers.

"Yes, it's beautiful. The Sun is shining and there are big puffy clouds in the sky," chattered the monkeys.

"And feel the wind—blowing just enough to keep us cool," said the mountain.

"And there's plenty of food and water for everyone," sang the birds.

Suddenly the Earth proclaimed, "It is time for us to vote for the Master of Weather. I'm sure you'll all agree that it

(continued on next page)

should be me, the Earth, who is made the Master. For without me, there would be no weather!"

All at once, huge black clouds filled the sky and the Sun disappeared behind them. The Air became frosty and the wind whipped through the trees and flowers. Then rain began pouring down and lightning flashed and thunder roared. In seconds it got so cold the rain changed to sleet and then to snow. And the wind blew harder and harder.

The lions and tigers and monkeys and birds all shivered and tried to keep warm. The trees and flowers were blown every which way. And the sand and dirt were tossed about in the wind.

"Please stop," begged the trees and the flowers.

"Yes, please," cried the rocks. "It's not our fault that the Earth is so vain."

"We know that without all four weather makers there would be no life and there would be no weather," the sand sputtered.

"Without Air, we animals and plants could not live," said the lions and ants and trees. "And there would be no wind.

"And without Water there would be no oceans, rivers, lakes, streams, puddles, clouds, or seas. And there would not be a drop of rain or a flake of snow. Why, there wouldn't even be animals or plants because we're all made of water!"

"And without the Sun, there would be no warmth and no sunshine to make the plants grow," said the trees. "And no heat to stir the winds and evaporate the water to make clouds."

"And, yes, the Earth is important too, for he gives us a place to live," whispered the butterflies, who were having a hard time in the blowing snow and winds. "We know the Earth rotates around the Sun and makes our seasons. And the Earth absorbs the heat from the Sun and keeps us warm."

"You are all the Masters of Weather," cried the animals, plants, mountain, rocks, and sand together.

Suddenly the Earth felt very ashamed. "I'm sorry, my friends. The Water, the Air, and the Sun are all just as important as

I am. For we are a weather team. I never thought about what it would be like without them. I have learned a lesson I will never forget."

And suddenly the wind stopped blowing and the rain stopped pouring. The Sun came out, smiling on all the inhabitants of the world. The celebration went on and on. And the four weather makers never had a disagreement again.

WEATHER MYTHS

Here are some suggestions for weather myths, stories, and fables. (In many myths, stories, and fables there are usually some truths mixed in with the story lines. Have the kids look up facts about their topics so they can include some in their stories.)

- How Rainbows Came to Be
- Why the Earth Spins on a Tilted Axis
- Why We Have Seasons
- Why Some Clouds Are White
- How Thunder Got Its Boom
- Why the Wind Blows
- Why Snowflakes Have Six Sides
- Why Air Is Invisible
- How the Sun Came to Be So Hot
- Where Raindrops Come From

BRANCHING OUT: ARTS AND CRAFTS

After reading "The Weather Master" to your group, try these activities:

- Have each person draw a picture of his or her favorite part of the story and hang the pictures up around the room.

- Divide the group into four teams: the Earth Team, the Sun Team, the Water Team, and the Air Team. Have each team make a collage composed of drawings, articles cut from newspapers, and photographs cut from magazines about how their weather maker affects the weather. For example, the Water Team might have pictures of clouds, rain, snow, floods, sleet, and umbrellas. And the Earth Team could have pictures of mountains, valleys, trees, and volcanoes.

A Hot Contest

Compare temperatures over different surfaces.

Objective:
Compare how different surfaces absorb sunlight.

Ages:
Primary

Materials:
- *6 thermometers*
- *6 Styrofoam cups*

Subject:
Science

Mountains, valleys, glaciers, forests, oceans, lakes, buildings, highways, ponds, lawns, and beaches are just a few of the features of the earth's surface. And each one absorbs different amounts of sunlight. Generally, darker surfaces absorb more sunlight than lighter ones. Different textures and shapes also influence the amount of sunlight absorbed.

The more sunlight a surface absorbs, the hotter it will get and the more the air just above the surface will heat up. In this activity, your group will find out how different surfaces affect the air temperatures above them.

Make a list of six different surfaces on the chalkboard or on a large piece of paper. For example, you might list blacktop, sand, soil, concrete, water, and grass. Tell the group that they will get to go outside to measure the air temperature over each surface. But first they have to guess which surface they think will be the warmest and which will be the coolest. Have each person write his or her guesses on a piece of paper.

Then divide them into six teams (one for each surface). Give each team a thermometer and a Styrofoam cup. If the thermometer has a backing, have them push the backing and the thermometer through the bottom of the cup. (If your thermometers don't have backings, have the kids poke pencils through the bottoms of their cups and then push the thermometers in from the bottom.) To take a measurement, have them set their cups on the ground, topside down.

Tell the teams they'll be taking two measurements, one in the sunlight and one in the shade. Have each team set a cup, topside down, over each of these surfaces. They should leave the cups in place for about five minutes, then write down the temperature readings of both thermometers.

When all the teams are finished, write the temperatures next to the list of surfaces. How well did the kids guess which were the warmest and which were the coolest surfaces? Explain that dark colors get warmer because they absorb more sunlight. That's why many people wear dark-colored clothes in winter and light-colored clothes in summer.

Balloons Around the Sun

Use balloons and a flashlight to simulate why the earth has seasons.

Objective:
Demonstrate how the earth's tilt affects weather patterns and our seasons.

Ages:
Primary and Intermediate

Materials:
- *balloons*
- *markers*
- *flashlight*
- *chalkboard or blacktop area*

(continued next page)

The earth is a sphere that never sits still. It is always spinning on a tilted axis (the spinning is what causes night and day) and it is always revolving around the sun at about 6500 miles (10,400 km) per hour. How do the earth's shape and its movements affect our weather? Since the earth is a sphere, the sun's energy falls on the earth unequally. Some areas get intense, direct sunlight; others get spread-out, weaker sunlight; and some areas, on the dark side, get none at all. This unequal heating causes differences in air temperatures and air pressures which cause the winds to blow.

Because the earth revolves around the sun at a tilt, different parts of the earth get different amounts of sunlight at different times of the year. This creates our seasons and explains why we have different weather patterns at different times of the year.

Here is a way to demonstrate how the earth's tilt and rotation affect our weather. First draw the diagram shown on the next page on the board or on the blacktop outside, showing how the earth revolves around the sun. Explain that the seasons keep changing because the tilt of the earth's axis is always at the same angle as the earth circles around the sun (see diagram on page 10). When the North Pole is tilted farthest away from the sun, North America is having the first day of winter and South America is having the first day

(continued on next page)

of summer. When the North Pole is tilted nearest to the sun, North America is having the first day of summer and South America is having the first day of winter.

You can also explain what the solstices and equinoxes are by using the diagram. The *summer solstice,* which is on June 20 or 21, marks the beginning of summer in the Northern Hemisphere. On this day, the noon sun is high in the sky and there are more hours of daylight than on any other day of the year. December 21 or 22 marks the beginning of winter in the Northern Hemisphere. This is the *winter solstice,* which means the noon sun is very low in the sky and there are fewer daylight hours than on any other day.

The *vernal equinox,* on March 20 or 21, marks the start of spring. And the *autumnal equinox* marks the beginning of autumn on September 22 or 23. On both the vernal and autumnal equinoxes, the sun is directly above the equator and the lengths of the day and night are nearly the same everywhere on earth. (On the first day of spring the North Pole begins to tilt toward the sun and on the first day of autumn it starts to tilt away again.)

After explaining the seasons and the earth's tilt using the diagram, have the kids "act out" the earth's revolution around the sun. Assign one person to be

the sun. Give the "sun" a flashlight. Then choose four other children to be earths. Have each "earth" blow up a large balloon. Then have them use black markers to draw a rough outline of North and South America on one side of their balloons.

Now have the earths station themselves at equal intervals around the sun. Have them walk around the sun holding the balloons with all the North Poles tilted toward the same point and North and South America always facing the sun.

When you say stop, have the sun point to one of the earths and walk over and shine the light on the balloon. (The sun needs to be fairly close to the earth so that the light will show up on the balloon, but not so close that it focuses on only one spot. Always keep the sun in the same position.) Ask the group if this represents spring, summer, fall, or winter in the Northern and Southern Hemispheres. (For example, if the earth were positioned so that the North Pole tilted farthest away from the sun, North America would be having the first day of winter and South America would be having the first day of summer. You could also see that when the North and South Poles get light, this light is always slanted and is never direct.)

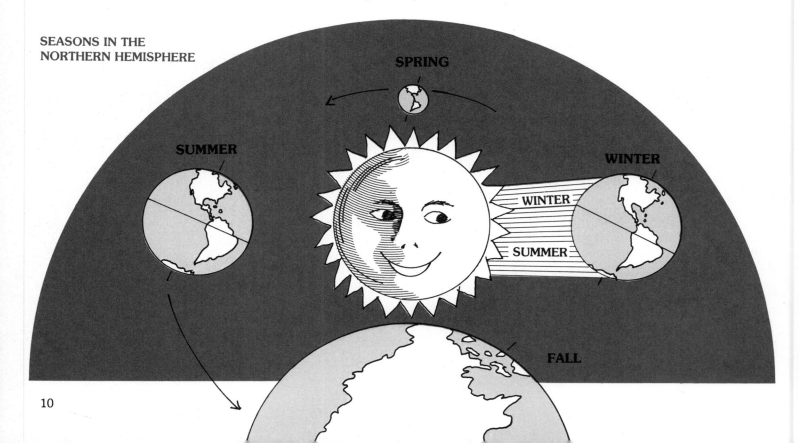

**SEASONS IN THE
NORTHERN HEMISPHERE**

SPRING

SUMMER

WINTER

WINTER

SUMMER

FALL

The Pressure Is On

Use balloons to show that air has weight.

Objective:
Demonstrate that air has weight and moves from an area of higher pressure to an area of lower pressure.

Ages:
Primary and Intermediate

Materials:
- balloons for each person
- 2 large balloons of equal size
- 2 yardsticks
- string
- pin
- books or other weights

Subject:
Science

ere are two quick and easy mini-experiments that help explain some of the properties of air.

MINI-EXPERIMENT #1: A WEIGHTY PROBLEM

Does air have weight? Ask your group what they think. If they say it does, ask them how they would prove it. If they don't know, tell them you can prove it does by using string, two balloons, and two yardsticks.

The first thing you need to do is make a yardstick balance. Lay one of the yardsticks on a high table or desk so that one end sticks way over the edge. Weight down the other end with books.

Then take a 12-inch (30-cm) piece of string and make a loop on each end. (Make the loops just big enough to slip over the ends of the yardsticks.) Slip one loop over the end of the yardstick that is sticking over the edge of the table. Then slip the other loop over the end of the other yardstick and move it toward the center until the yardstick hangs perfectly balanced (see diagram).

Next blow up two large balloons (make sure they are the same size) and tie them shut. Attach a 10-inch (25-cm) piece of string to the tied end of each balloon. Form a loop on the other end of each of the strings and slip the balloons on the yardstick balance—one on each end. Position the center string so that the yardstick is again balanced (see diagram).

Now slowly deflate one of the balloons by making a tiny hole with a pin near the knot. As the air rushes out, the balance will tip and the balloon that is still full of air will sink.

Ask the group what happened. (Because air has weight, the deflated balloon weighs less than it did before it lost all its air.)

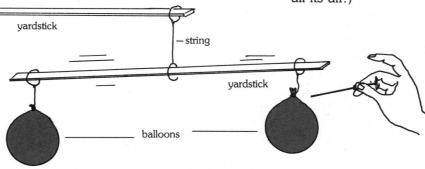

books / table / yardstick / string / yardstick / balloons

MINI-EXPERIMENT #2: THE BALLOON TRICK

Take the group outside and hand each person a large balloon. Tell the kids to blow up their balloons and hold onto them until everyone's balloon is full of air. (Don't tie the balloons.) Then, on the count of three, give the signal to have them release their balloons into the air. The balloons should go sailing around and finally plop to the ground.

After the kids retrieve their balloons, ask them what happened. What made the balloons zip away?

Explain that as they blew up their balloons, they forced air into a small, confined space. This put the air under high pressure. But the air outside the balloons was at a lower pressure. When the kids let their balloons go, the high-pressure air inside the balloons escaped to the low-pressure air on the outside. This is exactly what happens when the wind blows: Air moves from an area of higher pressure to an area of lower pressure.

Water on the Move

Make a mini-water cycle and write a water cycle adventure.

Objectives:
Observe the water cycle in a closed system. Describe the path a water droplet might follow over a period of ten days. Draw a diagram of the water cycle.

Ages:
Primary and Intermediate

Materials:
- *wide-mouth glass jars or drinking glasses*
- *a lawn*
- *paper*
- *pencils and crayons*
- *copies of page 14*

Subjects:
Language Arts and Science

Every second of the day, water is on the move—evaporating, condensing, and falling as rain, drizzle, snow, sleet, or hail. In the first part of this activity, your children will be able to see a miniature water cycle in action. And in the second part, they can create their own water cycle adventures.

GRASS UNDER GLASS

Here's a quick and easy way to show how water evaporates and condenses, two important parts of the water cycle. Try this on a sunny day.

Give each person a wide-mouth glass jar or drinking glass. Then take everyone outside to a thick green lawn. Have each person turn over his or her glass on the grass. In just a few minutes the children will begin to see water droplets form on the insides of their glasses—evidence that a mini-water cycle is at work.

What is happening? Grass is continually pulling water out of the soil and up into its stems and leaves. The water evaporates through the leaves into the air as water vapor. (The loss of water vapor to the air from leaves is called *transpiration*.) Normally water vapor disperses into the atmosphere. But in this experiment the vapor collects inside the jar until the air becomes *saturated* and can't hold any more. The additional water vapor then *condenses,* forming droplets on the jar. (Some water evaporates from the soil too. Have the kids try this experiment again by putting their glasses over patches of dirt. What happens?)

DRIPPY TALES

Sop the Drop bumped, bounced, and slid along the ground. "Ouch, ooooch!" he moaned. "This is the worst part of the whole trip." All around him other raindrops were falling to the ground and rushing down the hill. Sliding into one another, the droplets formed little rivulets and finally (it seemed to take forever) slid into the calm water of a warm farm pond.

So begins the tale of a water molecule's journey through the water cycle. If the story continued, Sop the Drop could evaporate into the atmosphere and be blown almost anywhere.

In this water cycle activity, your group will get a chance to invent their own raindrop characters and describe what happens to them on a trip through the water cycle.

Begin the activity by talking about how water recycles itself through oceans, streams, ponds, plants, animals, people, soil, clouds, and precipitation. Then pass out the water cycle maze on page 14 and have each person follow the path of the raindrop as it lands in a waterfall, plops into a pond, is drunk and excreted by a raccoon and a turtle, soaks into the soil, is "sucked up" by a tree, and finally evaporates into the air from the leaves of the tree to become part of a cloud again.

Once the group understands how the water cycle works, have them try to create their own waterdrop adventures. To give the children a time frame for their stories, tell them that if a waterdrop doesn't get "sidetracked" by becoming groundwater or ice, it will usually complete the water cycle in about ten days. Have them draw diagrams of their water cycles to illustrate their "drippy tales." (See "Drip the Drop," *Ranger Rick,* March 1983, pp. 12–14.)

The Weather Game

Play a word game to show how the sun, the earth, air, and water relate to weather.

Objective:
Describe several ways the earth, the sun, air, and water affect our weather.

Ages:
Intermediate and Advanced

Materials:
- *paper and pencils*
- *weather reference books (optional)*

Subject:
Science

ere's a word game that will get your group thinking about how the sun, the earth, water, and air are connected to our weather. You can use it as a follow-up to a discussion about how each of the four weather makers affects the weather. Or you can use it as a weather unit wrap-up, to see how well your group fits the "pieces of weather" together.

First pass out a game sheet to each person with the words *sun, air, water,* and *earth* written across the top and the word *weather* written down the left-hand side. (See the filled-in example below.)

THE OBJECT OF THE GAME

The object of the game is to fill in the spaces under each category (sun, earth, water, air) with words or phrases that relate the category topic to weather. The first space under each category has to be filled in with words that start with the letter "w." The words in the second space under each category must start with the letter "e," and so on.

There are no right or wrong answers in this game. If a child can explain how a word or phrase relates to weather and to the category, he or she gets credit for it. For example, under sun, you could have "wave" in the "w" space because the sun's energy travels to earth as solar waves.

By making the children think about each subject as it relates to weather, the game will help them better understand that all four categories—the sun, the earth, air, and water—are connected and interact to create our weather.

HOW TO SCORE

Explain the rules and have the children try to fill in as many spaces as they can. Give them a time limit and explain that they don't have to fill in *every* space. (It would be very hard to fill them all in.) Score ten points for each word or phrase that no one else has thought of, five points for those that others have also written, and zero points for a blank. The person with the most points at the end wins.

You can also make this a discussion activity and not keep score at all. And you can allow the group to use reference books to help them fill out their sheets. The only requirement is that each person must be able to explain the connections of his or her words to the category and to weather.

	SUN	EARTH	AIR	WATER
W	Wind	Winter	Weight	Water vapor
E	Enormous	Eruptions	Expands	Evaporates
A	Angle of rays	Absorbs heat	Atmosphere	Acid rain
T	Temperature	Tilted axis	Troposphere	Thunderheads
H	Heat	Horse latitudes	Humidity	Hail
E	Energy	Exhausts	Exosphere	Electricity
R	Radiation	Rotates	Relative humidity	Rain

COPYCAT PAGE

Take Sop the Drop on a trip through the water cycle!

Start Here

You Did It!

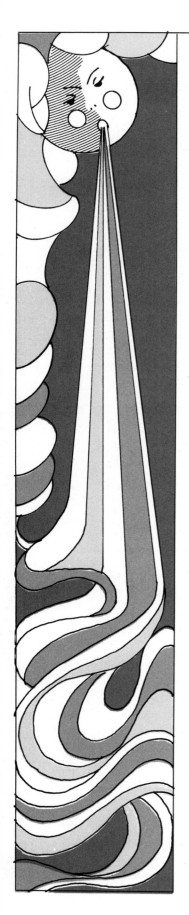

A windy day is great for flying kites, sailing boats, scattering seeds, and spinning pinwheels. But sometimes the wind goes wild, knocking over trees, blowing down buildings, and causing huge ocean waves to swell. All of these winds are nothing more than air on the move.

Air always tries to flow from an area of high pressure to an area of lower pressure. (Think of the way air rushes out of a balloon when you open the end. The air from the high pressure area inside the balloon flows to an area of lower pressure outside.) If there is a big difference in air pressure from one area to another, then strong, gusting winds will blow. But if there is only a small difference in pressure, the winds will be light and breezy.

Winds You Can Count On: There are some wind patterns in the world that happen over and over, nearly all the time. These winds blow in the same general direction and are called *prevailing winds*. There are three major belts of prevailing winds in the Northern and Southern Hemispheres:

- **Trade Winds**—These winds blow toward the equator from the northeast in the Northern Hemisphere and the southeast in the Southern Hemisphere. European sailing vessels used to depend on trade winds to bring them to the New World.
- **Prevailing Westerlies**—These winds blow more from west to east than from north or south across the middle latitudes of the Northern and Southern Hemispheres. The United States and parts of Canada are in the path of the prevailing westerlies, which is why our weather systems usually move from west to east.
- **Polar Easterlies**—These cold winds blow from the North (or South) Pole and move south and west (or north and east) until they reach the region of the prevailing westerlies. When this cold air meets warmer air, windy and rainy weather often occurs.

Blow East, Blow West: Because the earth spins, the winds of the world are deflected as they blow. This is called the *Coriolis Effect*. In the Northern Hemisphere, the winds are deflected to the right. And in the Southern Hemisphere, they are deflected to the left. (The Coriolis Effect has a lot to do with making the prevailing winds blow in the direction they do.)

Winds in Special Places: Many places around the world have their own special regional and local winds that are influenced by mountains, oceans, valleys, and other features of the earth's surface, as well as by the way the atmosphere is layered. Here are just a few:

- **Monsoons**—These are seasonal winds that blow toward a continent in summer and away from a continent in winter. The monsoons in Asia are the most famous. In summer they bring huge rainstorms from the Indian Ocean. In winter they bring dry weather. Monsoons are caused by great temperature differences between the land and the ocean.

(continued on next page)

- **Mountain Winds**—Chinooks, mistrals, zondas, and williwaws are just a few of the names for winds that form over mountain ranges around the world. For example, *chinooks* are warm, dry winds that blow down from the slopes of the Rocky Mountains in the United States and Canada. Many people call them "snow-eaters" because they bring warm weather that quickly melts and sometimes even evaporates snow.

- **Sea Breezes and Land Breezes**—Near any large body of water you can often feel breezes blowing during the day and night. Here's what happens:

   When the sun beats down during the day, the land heats more quickly than the water does. The hot land warms the air above it more quickly than the water can. The warmer air is lighter and it rises. Cooler air from over the water moves in to replace the rising warm air and creates a *sea* or *lake breeze*.

   At night, the land loses heat more quickly than the water does. So the wind blows from the cooler land to the warmer water. This is called a *land breeze*.

- **Jet Streams**—Jet streams are strong, fast-moving rivers of air high in our atmosphere. They are caused by huge temperature differences in the atmosphere. Jet streams can blow well over 100 miles (160 km) per hour and may cause major shifts in weather patterns.

Domes of Air in the Sky: A huge volume of air with about the same temperature and humidity throughout is called an *air mass*. An air mass, which is shaped like a big, upside-down bowl, can be hundreds or thousands of miles across.

Air masses form in tropical and polar areas where huge volumes of air sit for days or even weeks. As the air sits there, it gets warmer or cooler, wetter or drier, depending on the characteristics of the land or water beneath it.

Air Masses on the Move: Huge waves of air high in the atmosphere are what steer air masses and "push" them along. Just like enormous waves of water in the ocean, these waves of air can be thousands of miles long. As air masses move, they move as a whole body, bringing certain weather conditions with them. (The weather conditions of an air mass can change as it moves over different surfaces.)

'Tis the Season: At different times of the year our weather is influenced by air masses that form in different areas. For example, in winter, polar air masses from the north bring cold, often dry weather. But in the summer, tropical air masses from the south often bring warm, humid, or stormy weather.

Weather Up Front: Where two air masses of different temperatures and/or humidities meet, a *weather front* forms. The front is a boundary between the two air masses. But instead of mixing as water and orange juice concentrate do, one air mass pushes over or under the other one.

- **Cold Fronts: When Cold Hits Warm**—When a cold air mass pushes into a warm air mass, the cold air digs under the lighter air of the warm air mass. As the cold air slips under the warm air, it pushes the warm air up, causing it to cool. If there's enough moisture, clouds may form and rain or snow may fall. If really cold and dry air pushes into very warm and moist air, the weather can become violent. Huge thunderstorms and even tornadoes may form along the leading edge of cold air, where the warm humid air is being rapidly pushed up.

When a cold air mass pushes against a warm air mass, the boundary between the two air masses is called a cold front. The symbol for a cold front is: ▼▼▼

WARM FRONT

COLD AIR

WARM AIR

COLD FRONT

WARM AIR

COLD AIR

- **Warm Fronts: When Warm Hits Cold**—The weather also changes when warm air moves in to replace retreating colder air. The warm air (which is lighter than the cold air) climbs over the sloping sides of the colder, denser air of the cold air mass. This gradual uplift cools the warm moist air and often produces clouds and rain, drizzle, or snow.

When a warm air mass replaces a cold air mass, the boundary between the two air masses is called a **warm front.** *The symbol for a warm front is:*

Blow High, Blow Low: Weather forecasters look not only at the temperature and humidity of the air to predict the weather—they also look at the air pressure that is exerted on the surface of the earth. An area of high pressure is called a *High* and an area of low pressure is called a *Low.* Highs and Lows share these characteristics:
- the air pressure is highest or lowest at their centers
- they usually have roughly circular shapes
- their sizes can range from less than 100 miles (160 km) to more than a thousand miles (1600 km) in diameter
- the air moves in a spiral within each system

Highs and Lows are *different* in these ways:

Highs
- also called *anti-cyclones*
- the air moves clockwise in a spiral outward from the center
- *usually* bring clear and fair weather
- the pressure is highest at their centers

Lows
- also called *cyclones*
- the air moves counterclockwise in a spiral toward the center
- *usually* bring cloudy and stormy weather
- the pressure is lowest at their centers

Fitting Them All Together: So how do air masses, fronts, Highs, and Lows all fit together? Here are some of the relationships that show how they can all connect:
- Air masses usually have high pressure systems at their centers.
- When two air masses of different temperatures meet, their common border, called a *front,* is a place where warm air is rising. As the rising warm air expands and cools, it can produce clouds and stormy weather.
- Most low pressure systems form along the boundaries (fronts) between air masses.
- Currents of air in the upper atmosphere steer air masses along. These currents move with a wavelike motion.
- Moving weather systems transfer energy, some in the form of heat, from one area to another. Without storms and moving air masses, the tropics would get incredibly hot and the polar regions would get incredibly cold.
- As air masses move across North America, they bring changing weather conditions. By understanding how these air masses and the High and Low systems that are associated with them are different, you can make general forecasts about the weather coming to your area.

The Ways of the Wind

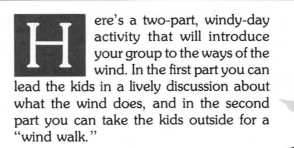

Take a wind walk and discuss how wind affects living things.

Objectives:
Name several things the wind can move. List several ways people use the wind. Give examples of how the wind can help plants and animals.

Ages:
Primary

Materials (part 1):
- *leaves*
- *rock (about the size of a softball or larger)*
- *sand or small pebbles*
- *part of a plant that's gone to seed, such as a milkweed pod, dandelion flower head, or cattail*
- *flower (or a picture of one)*
- *pictures of a spider, a mushroom, and a lion or other predator*

Materials (part 2):
- *warm water*
- *glycerine*
- *dish detergent*
- *sugar*
- *copies of page 24*
- *pipe cleaners*
- *leakproof container*

Subject:
Science

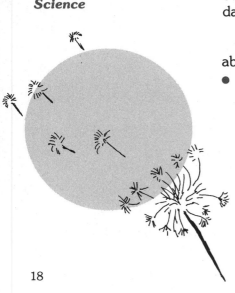

Here's a two-part, windy-day activity that will introduce your group to the ways of the wind. In the first part you can lead the kids in a lively discussion about what the wind does, and in the second part you can take the kids outside for a "wind walk."

WHAT DOES THE WIND DO?

Before the children arrive, gather together a few seeds and leaves, some sand, and a rock to use in a discussion. You can also cut pictures from magazines. (See the list of materials for suggestions of things to use.)

When you are ready to start, have all the kids sit in a circle. Ask them to name some of the ways people use the wind. (Wind helps people fly kites, sail boats, dry clothes, power windmills, and go hang gliding and windsurfing.) Then hold up the objects and pictures one at a time and talk about how the wind affects each one.

For younger children, start by holding up a leaf and asking if they think the wind can blow a leaf away. When do a lot of leaves get blown around by the wind? (in the fall or before a thunderstorm) Next hold up a rock. Do the kids think the wind could blow the rock away? Explain that it would take a strong wind to make the rock move! Then pass around some sand or small pebbles. Ask if the wind could blow the sand or pebbles. Then ask if they have ever been to the beach on a very windy day.

Here are some other things you can talk about:

- **Seeds:** Hold up part of a plant that's gone to seed. (Milkweed pods, dandelion flower heads, and cattails will all work well.) Can the kids say how the wind can help the plant? Try blowing some of the seeds to show how the wind carries them to different places.

Explain that the wind spreads the seeds to new places to grow. When the seeds sprout, the young plants won't all be crowded together in the same place.

- **Pollen:** Besides carrying seeds, the wind can also carry a plant's pollen. Show the kids a flower (or a picture of one) as you talk about wind and pollen.

- **Spores:** Show the kids a picture of a mushroom and explain that mushrooms, like all fungi, grow from tiny spores. Just like the seeds of many plants, spores can sail on the wind to new places.

- **Spiders:** A lot of spiders can use the wind to help them move around. As you hold up a picture of a spider, tell the group that young spiders will often climb to a high place and spin a thin thread of silk. When the wind blows, it catches the silken line and carries the spider to a new area. (This is called *ballooning.*)

- **Predators and Prey:** Show the children a picture of a lion, fox, or some other predatory mammal. How can the wind help an animal that hunts other animals? Explain that the wind carries odors that help a predator sniff out its prey. How could the wind help a deer or a rabbit? (It might bring a predator's scent to the animal in time for it to escape.)

While the children are thinking about all the things wind can do, take them outside for a walk in the wind.

WIND WALK

Once you and your group are out in the breeze, ask them how they can tell it's a windy day. The obvious answer is that they can feel the wind blowing. But as you walk along, have them look for other windy day "clues." Point out blowing leaves, swirling dust, swaying branches, waving flags, and other windblown things. You may also want to have the kids lie on their backs and look up at the sky to find another clue—moving clouds. They might see that the wind near the ground sometimes blows in a different direction from the wind high up in the atmosphere. *Warning: When the children lie down, make sure they face a direction that will keep them from looking directly into the sun.*

A nice way to end a wind walk is to have the kids blow bubbles and watch which way the wind takes them. Just bring some "magic bubble mix" (see recipe below) along with you as you walk. Also bring along some bubble dippers and a pan to pour the mixture into. To make a bubble dipper, twist one pipe cleaner into a loop and attach it to another pipe cleaner. Curl any sharp ends out of the way.

As a follow-up to the activity, pass out copies of page 24 for the kids to work on. When they are finished, have the kids tell how the animals and plants they drew are affected by the wind.

MAGIC BUBBLE MIX

- 3 cups warm water
- 8 tablespoons glycerine (available at most drugstores)
- 8 tablespoons liquid dish detergent
- 1 dash sugar

Put everything together in a leakproof container and shake thoroughly. Your magic bubble mix is ready!

Crazy Hot Air Balloons

Make a hot air balloon.

Objective:
Observe that hot air rises.

Ages:
Primary and Intermediate

Materials:
- *7 sheets of 20 × 30" (50 × 75-cm) tissue paper*
- *5 soup, frozen juice, or coffee cans (all with the same diameter)*
- *lightweight wire (3–4" [8–10 cm] longer than the circumference of the cans)*
- *camp stove and fuel (A compact, propane stove with 6–8" [15–20 cm] legs works best.)*
(continued next page)

Using tissue paper and glue, your kids can make their own hot air balloons. It's a great way to show that hot air rises. (See page 20 for Figures 1–8.)

1. Place one sheet of 20 × 30-inch (50 × 75-cm) tissue paper on top of another. Fold the pieces in half as shown in Figure 1 and cut along the fold. This will make four pieces of tissue paper, each measuring 15 × 20 inches (38 × 50 cm).
2. Stack the four halves evenly. Position the stack so the 20-inch (50-cm) sides are at the top and bottom. Fold the pieces in half, then fold them in half a second time in the same direction.
3. Open the last fold you made and make a diagonal fold along the line shown in Figure 2. Be sure to make the fold along the margin that is *not* closed. Cut along the diagonal fold line. When you unfold the sheets,

they should look like the drawing in Figure 3. *(continued next page)*

Bruce Norfleet

- *matches*
- *scissors and glue*
- *clear tape and duct tape*
- *thick gloves or pot-holder mittens*

Subjects:
Science and Crafts

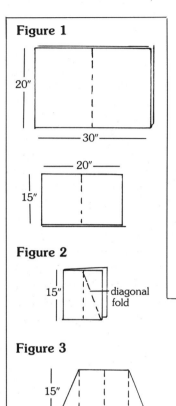

Figure 1

20″

30″

Figure 2

20″

15″

15″ — diagonal fold

Figure 3

15″

20″

Figure 4

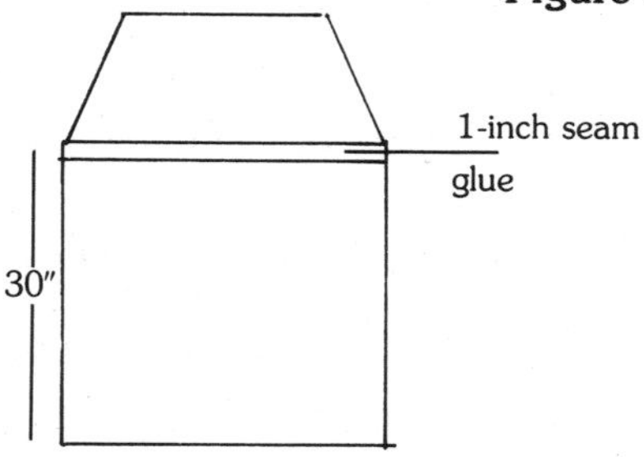

1-inch seam
glue

30″

Figure 5

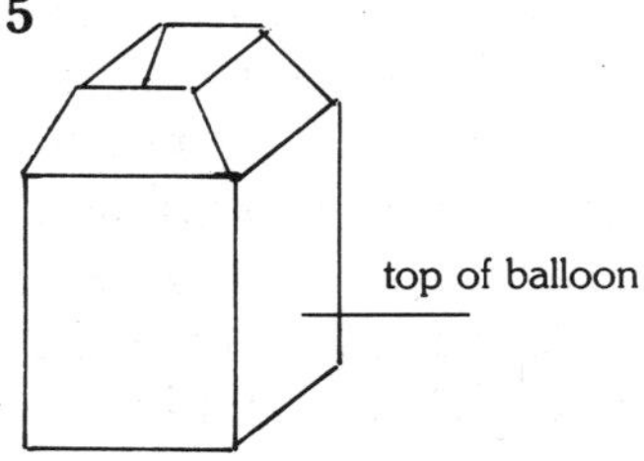

top of balloon

4. Take one of the sheets you just made and glue it to a sheet of 20 × 30-inch (50 × 75-cm) tissue paper, as shown in Figure 4. (Use the glue sparingly and make the 1-inch [2.5-cm] seam along the 20-inch [50-cm] side of the sheet.) Do the same for each sheet, making four balloon sides.

5. Making 1-inch (2.5-cm) seams again, glue the edges of the sides together so that your balloon looks like the drawing in Figure 5.

6. To make a top for the balloon, take the last sheet of 20 × 30-inch tissue paper and cut a 10 × 20-inch (25 × 50-cm) strip from one end. (See Figure 6.)

7. Glue all four sides of the 20 × 20-inch (50 × 50-cm) square top to the sides of the balloon's larger opening.

8. Bend the lightweight wire into a circle that fits loosely around one of the cans, and then twist the ends together. (See Figure 7.)

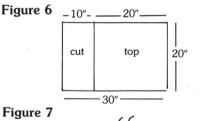

Figure 6

— 10″ — ——— 20″ ———

cut   top   20″

30″

Figure 7

twist ends

Figure 8

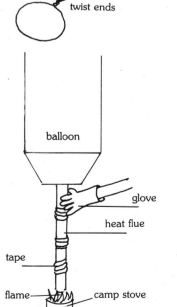

balloon

glove

heat flue

tape

flame — camp stove

propane

9. Place the wire circle just inside the balloon's smaller opening. Fold the surrounding tissue paper over the wire and tape in place with clear tape.

10. To make a heat flue for filling the balloon with hot air, cut out the ends of five cans. (Be careful of the sharp edges!) Be sure all the diameters of the cans are the same size. (A diameter of 3 inches [7.5 cm] works well.) Remove any paper labels from the cans by soaking them in hot water. Dry the outsides of the cans, stack one on top of another, and tape them together with plenty of duct tape. (Cardboard frozen juice cans can be used instead of metal cans to make a flue.)

11. *Caution:* Before launching the balloon, read *Hot Tips.* Then hold the flue over the heat source and lower the wire-ringed end of the balloon over the top end of the flue. Let the balloon fill with hot air until it will rise on its own. (See Figure 8.)

HOT TIPS

- Each balloon may be decorated or personalized with streamers or markers. But remind your group that any extra weight may slow the balloons down.
- Find a launch site in an open area away from trees, electrical cables, and power lines. Picnic tables make good launching platforms.
- Since the balloon is highly flammable, an adult should take charge of the heat source. Older students may handle the flue with thick gloves or pot holders, and younger ones can help hold the balloon in place before lift-off.
- Be sure to avoid placing the flue directly in the flame.
- Cool, calm days are the best for flying. Wind will quickly cool the balloons and may blow them away. And the balloons will have a hard time getting started on hot, humid days.

Idea by Dr. Milton Payne, Box 1307, Stephen F. Austin State University, Nacogdoches, TX 75962. Instructions reprinted with permission.

Follow the Front

Make a paper model of a warm front and a cold front.

Objectives:
Explain what a front is. Define the terms warm front *and* cold front.

Ages:
Intermediate and Advanced

Materials:
- *copies of page 25*
- *scissors*
- *several blue crayons*
- *tape or glue*
- *paper or thin cardboard*

Subject:
Science

Fronts can bring some messy weather—but usually not without warning. As a front approaches, certain cloud patterns form. By keeping an eye on these clouds, you can get a good idea of what the weather will be like later in the day or the next day.

Pass out copies of page 25 and have your kids make their own "front viewers" to help them understand the cloud patterns that go along with fronts. Here's how to do it:

1. Cut out the three large strips along the dotted lines. Also cut out the "city."
2. Color the cold air blue.
3. Tape or glue the strips together by matching up the letters. For example, match up the letters A and tape. Then match up the letters B and tape.
4. To make the viewer itself, fold a piece of paper or thin cardboard in half lengthwise and make a vertical 2½-inch (6-cm) cut about 2 inches (5 cm) from the right-hand edge and ¾ inch (2 cm) from the bottom edge. Then make another cut about 3 inches (7.5 cm) away from the first one (see diagram).
5. Tape or glue the city below the two slits.
6. Now feed the strip through the two slits. (Pull it through from left to right so that you start with Monday morning.)

Once the children finish putting everything together, lead a brief discussion about fronts. (See page 16 in the background information.) Have the children slowly pull their front strips through the viewers to see how clouds can tell us about approaching fronts.

Later, the children can use what they've learned about fronts and clouds to try to predict when a warm or cold front will come their way. Have them observe the clouds each day to come up with a prediction. Then discuss what happens, "front-wise," each day.

Note: In this activity, we have listed typical warm and cold front weather patterns. But in many areas, especially along coasts, these patterns might be different. Check with a local meteorologist to find out about the front patterns in your area.

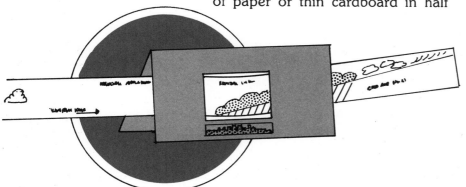

Warm Front Follies

Put on a warm front mini-play.

Objectives:
Explain what a warm front is. Name two types of clouds associated with a warm front.

Ages:
Intermediate and Advanced

Materials:
- *copies of the mini-play on page 22*

(continued next page)

When a front moves your way, you can count on several other weather "events" to occur along with it. For example, clouds—sometimes three or four different kinds of them—move ahead of the front. Temperatures rise or fall when the front passes, depending on whether the front is warm or cold. And most of the time, some kind of precipitation develops ahead of the front or as the front passes overhead. By playing parts in the mini-play that follows, your children can get a feel for the events associated with a typical warm front. (You can also try the activity with a cold front—but there will be fewer parts.)

Before you start the play, talk a little about fronts in general. (See the background information on page 16.) You can often tell when a front is heading your way by looking at the clouds. For example, as a warm front approaches, high, wispy clouds called cirrus clouds usually move overhead first. Later come the lower, denser sheets of altostratus clouds. And then come the rainy nimbostratus clouds in a broad band just ahead of the front itself. (See the Cloud Chart insert.)

(continued on next page)

Now tell the kids they'll be acting out some of the different things that happen when a warm front forms. First print the numbers 1 through 9 on separate slips of paper. Then divide your kids into nine groups and let each group pick one number out of a hat.

Next pass out a copy of the mini-play (below) to each person and explain that each group will act out one of the numbered lines. For example, the group that drew number 1 out of the hat will play the part of the cold air mass (the first line of the play). The group that drew number 2 will play the part of the sun (the second line), and so on. Explain to the kids that the rhythm of the play is like that of "The House That Jack Built." Each line in it is based on the line that comes before it and everything is connected to everything else.

Starting with Group One, have each group come up to the front of the room and recite their particular line. (Have the groups line up in order, side by side.) Each time a new group comes up to say their line, all previous groups must say theirs too, in turn. For example, Group Four would come up and say: "We are the altostratus clouds that moved in below the . . ." and Group Three would pick up with, ". . . cirrus clouds so high in the sky, which passed in front of the . . ." Then Group Two would fill in their part, and Group One would add their line last. Explain to the kids that the word in their line that's in bold type is the word they start with each time (except the first time).

Encourage the kids to use their imaginations for their particular parts. For example, they may want to make simple costumes by cutting out construction paper pictures and hanging them around their necks with yarn. And they may want to add a little drama to their parts. For example, the cold air mass group could shiver, the cirrus cloud group could move gracefully, and the nimbostratus cloud group could make raining motions with their fingers.

Try the mini-play several times so the kids can really begin to understand what happens when a warm front passes through.

THE WARM FRONT FOLLIES MINI-PLAY

Bruce Norfleet

1. We are the **cold** air mass that hung around_____.
   (Say the name of your town, street, school, camp, or nature center.)
2. Here is the **sun** that shone down through the . . .
3. We are the **cirrus** clouds so high in the sky, which passed in front of the . . .
4. We are the **altostratus** clouds that moved in below the . . .
5. We are the **warm** wind that bumped into the cold air mass and formed the front that pushed along the . . .
6. We are the **nimbostratus** clouds brought by the . . .
7. We are the **rain** that fell from the . . .
8. We are the **warm** air that followed the front that brought the . . .
9. Here is the sun that shines again through the . . .

Windblown Poetry

The wind makes a great subject for poetry. Have your kids capture their impressions of the wind and the many forms it can take by writing their own wind poems.

To get them into a "windy" frame of mind, first list all the adjectives they can think of that can describe the "moods" of the wind. For example, you might list the words *gentle, warm, brisk, gusty, bitter, violent, dancing, blowing, soothing, cooling,* and *raging.* Then read a few wind poems by well-known poets and authors. Here is one by Mary O'Neill, from her book, *Winds* (Doubleday, 1970):

WIND PICTURES

Look! There's a giant stretching in the
  sky,
A thousand white-maned horses flying
  by,
A house, a mother mountain with her
  hills,
A lazy lady posing in her frills,
Cotton floating from a thousand bales,
And a white ship with white sails.

See the old witch fumbling with her shawl,
White towers piling on a castle wall,
The bits of soft that break and fall away,
Air-borne mushrooms with undersides of
  gray—
Above, a white doe races with her fawn
On the white grass of a celestial lawn.
Lift up your lovely heads and look
As wind turns clouds into a picture book.

A good way to start the children off is to have them write a *haiku* (HI-koo). A haiku is a Japanese form of verse with three lines. The first and third lines have five syllables and the second line has seven. One idea behind haiku is that it captures the writer's first reaction to something in nature, such as a sunset, a waterfall, or a flying bird. Here's an example of a wind haiku:

Gentle, caressing
Soft breeze plays among birch leaves
Friendly wind blowing

Cinquain (sing-CANE) is another type of poetry your kids can try. Cinquain consists of five lines, each of which has a special purpose. Here's the basic form of cinquain:
- first line states the title in two syllables
- second line describes the title in four syllables
- third line describes action in six syllables
- fourth line expresses a feeling in eight syllables
- fifth line restates the title in two syllables

Wind really lends itself to cinquain poetry. Read these examples to the children to get them started:

Breezes
Warm and flowing
Make flowers and limbs sway
Always touching and surrounding
Gentle

Cyclone
Ripping, raging
Swirling funnel of death
Struggling against the violence
Terror

Once the kids have the hang of writing wind poetry, have them branch out to other weather subjects. Clouds, fog, storms, and snow all have a lot of poetry potential. When everyone's finished writing, have the kids read their poems to the rest of the group. You could also have them make poem posters by writing their poems on index cards, drawing pictures that fit their poems, and pasting the index cards to the pictures. Hang the posters around the room or on a bulletin board.

It's a windy day in the country! Draw an animal and a plant that the wind "helps."

COPYCAT PAGE

FOLLOW THE FRONT

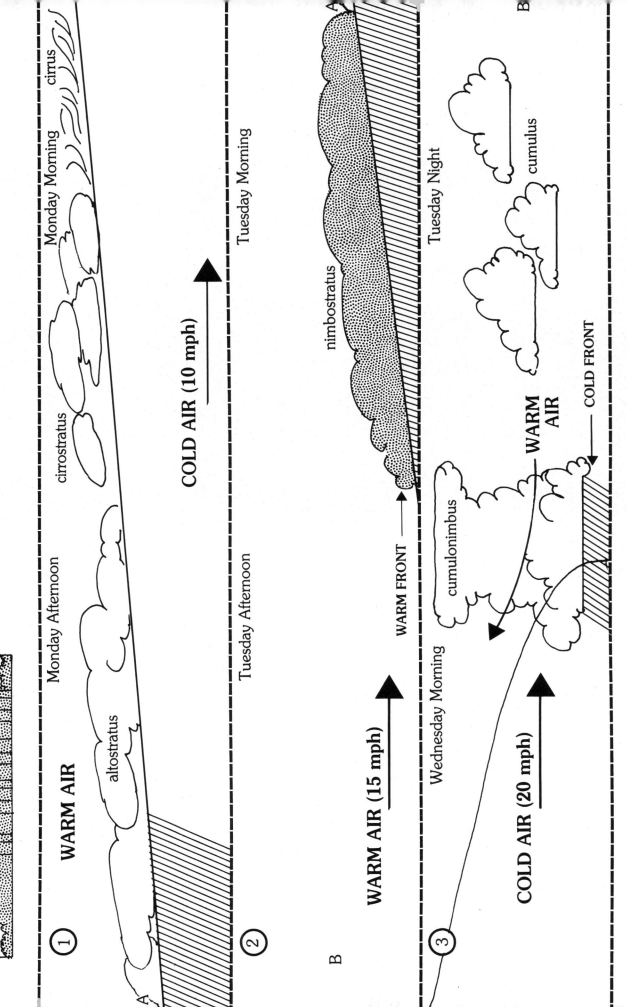

100 miles

City

① WARM AIR

Monday Morning — cirrus

Monday Afternoon

cirrostratus

altostratus

A

② COLD AIR (10 mph)

Tuesday Morning

Tuesday Afternoon

B

nimbostratus

WARM FRONT →

WARM AIR (15 mph)

③ COLD AIR (20 mph)

Tuesday Night

cumulus

cumulonimbus

WARM AIR

COLD FRONT

Wednesday Morning

B

RANGER RICK'S NATURESCOPE: WILD ABOUT WEATHER

MILD AND WILD WEATHER

The sun disappears quickly behind piles of darkening clouds. The clouds heap on top of each other, getting darker and bigger by the minute. A rush of cool air sweeps by. Suddenly lightning flashes, followed by a loud clap of thunder. And torrents of rain begin to fall. Thunderstorms like this, as well as hurricanes, tornadoes, blizzards, drizzle, hail, and other types of precipitation, are all connected with clouds.

Clouds are made up of billions of tiny water droplets or ice crystals that have formed around tiny particles in the air. A cloud forms when water *evaporates* (changes from a liquid to a gas) from the surface of the earth and then *condenses* (changes from a gas to a liquid) on dust specks, pollen, salt crystals, and other tiny particles found in the air.

A Cloud by Any Other Name: One way clouds are grouped is by the way they look. Each type of cloud has a descriptive Latin name. For example, *cumulo,* which means "pile" in Latin, gives us *cumulus* clouds, which look like piled-up heaps of cotton. Other Latin words used in naming clouds are: *cirro* (curl), *alto* (middle), *nimbus* (rain), and *stratus* (layered). Many types of clouds, such as *cumulonimbus,* have combination names because they have a combination of characteristics. Cumulonimbus clouds are towering thunderstorm clouds that pile up in the sky.

Clouds are also grouped according to where they form in the atmosphere. For example, cirrus clouds are high-sky clouds, while stratus clouds are low-sky clouds.

The droplets or ice crystals in a cloud are very, very tiny—about 70 times smaller than the period at the end of this sentence.

The Pitter-Patter of Precipitation: Rain, snow, sleet, hail, drizzle, and other forms of precipitation all fall from clouds—but only from certain kinds of clouds and only under certain conditions. And *how* the precipitation forms depends on the temperature of the cloud.

- *Cold Cloud Precipitation*—In our latitudes, most precipitation begins in clouds that are very cold. These clouds contain a mixture of ice crystals and supercooled water droplets. (The water droplets are below freezing, but still exist as a liquid.) In this environment, the supercooled water droplets evaporate. As the droplets evaporate and change into water vapor, the vapor "sticks" to the ice crystals, freezes, and makes the crystals grow larger.

    In a very short time, the crystals grow big and heavy enough to fall through the clouds. As they fall, they collide with and stick to more water droplets and ice crystals, and keep growing bigger.

    If these crystals fall through warm temperatures on their way to the ground, they melt into rain. But if the air above the ground is near or below freezing, the crystals will land as snow instead of rain.

Most of the rain that falls in North America begins as ice crystals. Even in the middle of summer the heavy rain from thunderstorms was first ice high up in the thunderclouds.

- **Warm Cloud Precipitation**—In lower latitudes, where the climate is tropical, the clouds are warmer. There are often no ice crystals in these warm clouds—just water droplets of all different sizes. These cloud droplets begin to collide and stick together. As the droplets become larger, they fall faster. Because they are of different sizes, the droplets fall at different speeds. And as they fall, they collide with more droplets in the cloud and get bigger and heavier. Finally, they are so large they fall as rain.

A raindrop contains a million times more water than a tiny cloud droplet!

Skies Alive with Rain: In most places, rain is the most common type of precipitation. It usually falls from nimbostratus, altostratus, and cumulonimbus clouds.

Contrary to what most people think, raindrops are not tear-shaped blobs of water. Large drops actually look more like tiny round pillows flattened on their bottoms and tops as they fall through the air. And smaller drops are spherical.

The Dampness of Drizzle and Mist: Drizzle falls to the ground from low stratus clouds. Since it forms in low clouds, the droplets don't have time to get as big as normal-sized raindrops that fall from higher and thicker clouds. The droplets in drizzle are so small they fall very slowly and seem to float in the air.

The Ways of Glaze: Glaze, which is clear ice, forms when cold rain or drizzle hits cold surfaces and freezes on contact. If the precipitation is heavy enough or lasts a long time, roads, trees, telephone lines, and everything else can get coated with a thick layer of ice. An ice storm like this causes a lot of damage when power lines and tree branches snap from the weight of the ice.

How to Know Snow: Snowflakes have six sides, just as ice crystals do. At warmer temperatures, when there is a lot of water vapor in the air, snowflakes are larger and tend to stick together in clumps. This "wet snow" makes great snowballs and snowpeople. At very low temperatures, snowflakes are smaller, making snow harder and more grainy. This "powder" is great for skiing. (For more about the different kinds of snow, see *The Secret Language of Snow* by Terry Tempest Williams and Ted Major; Sierra Club, 1984.)

Sleet: Sleet is made of hard, round beads of ice that are about the same size as raindrops. Sleet forms when rain falls through a thick layer of very cold air and freezes before reaching the ground.

Hurling Hailstones: Hailstones form in violent thunderstorms. They begin in clouds as small clusters of ice crystals. As the crystals fall through areas of supercooled cloud droplets, they can form "onionlike" layers of ice. Some hailstones can get as big as softballs before they crash into the ground.

Dew Does Not Fall: Tiny droplets of water that you see on plants in the morning are called dew. The dew does not come from clouds or from fog. It is formed when water vapor near the ground condenses at night, causing droplets to form on all exposed, cool surfaces. (See "Dewdrop Insects," *Ranger Rick,* May 1984, pp. 18–21.)

(continued on next page)

Listening to Lightning: As lightning travels, it heats the air in its path very quickly. This quick heating causes air to expand suddenly. As the air expands along the path of the lightning bolt, it vibrates, sending out sound waves that we hear as thunder.

Since lightning follows a zigzag path, the sound from a lightning stroke may reach us at different times. And that's why the thunder "rumbles."

The Shortest Route: Lightning tries to find the shortest path to the earth, and that means it will usually strike the highest grounded object in the area. Lightning rods protect buildings by providing a safe path for the lightning.

Dangerous Downpours: Flash floods from even nonviolent thunderstorms can cause dangerous conditions. Rivers, streams, and drainage ditches can turn into raging currents in a very short time—ripping up trees, knocking out bridges, and washing away homes.

Tornadoes Bring Big Troubles: Tornadoes are the most violent of all storms, with spiraling winds that can whirl faster than 200 miles (320 km) per hour. (It's hard to measure the actual speeds of the winds inside a tornado because the instruments can't survive such strong winds.)

Tornadoes are dark, funnel-shaped clouds that reach down to the earth's surface from cumulonimbus clouds. Most tornadoes don't last more than a few minutes; a few last as long as an hour. But during their short lifetimes they can do millions of dollars' worth of damage and take many lives.

The violent winds in a tornado can blow down trees and rip apart buildings, as well as send bricks, nails, pieces of wood, and other debris sailing through the air like missiles at over 100 miles (160 km) per hour. (See "Screamin' Demons," *Ranger Rick,* March 1984, pp.13–15, for more about tornadoes.)

The Wild Winds of Hurricanes: Hurricanes are capable of doing more damage than all other kinds of storms put together. That's because their destructive winds cover large areas and they bring torrential rains and devastating storm surges—huge surges of water from the rising ocean.

Most hurricanes sweep into the mainland United States from the Atlantic Ocean, the Gulf of Mexico, and the Caribbean Sea. They form in the hot, moist air masses that cover tropical oceans. Hurricanes that form in other parts of the world have different names. In Australia they are called *tropical cyclones,* in Asia *typhoons,* and in India *cyclones.*

The winds of a hurricane spiral in toward the center of the storm, which is called the *eye.* The air is relatively calm in the *eye* itself, which can be 15–30 miles (24–48 km) wide. But the *eye* is surrounded by a towering wall of dense clouds that produces most of the pounding rain and high winds. Sometimes the winds inside a hurricane whip around at over 150 miles (240 km) per hour. (Winds of over 74 miles [117 km] per hour are defined as hurricane winds.)

Hurricanes are huge storm systems, some of which are over 500 miles (800 km) wide.

Blizzards: Blinding snowstorms with howling winds and very cold temperatures are called *blizzards.* To be classified as a true blizzard, the winds must be over 35 miles (56 km) per hour and the visibility must be ¼ of a mile (0.4 km) or less. So much snow blows around during a blizzard that it is often impossible to see, and houses, cars, and animals can quickly become covered under huge snowdrifts.

Make a Weather Wheel

Keep track of each day's weather with a weather wheel.

Objective:
Observe and describe changes in the local weather.

Ages:
Primary

Materials:
- *cardboard*
- *magazine pictures of weather, or construction paper and crayons*
- *scissors*
- *paste*
- *big paper fastener*

Subject:
Science

Watching the weather change is the first step in understanding how it works. To help your children become aware of the weather and its daily changes, make a *weather wheel.* Here's how to do it:

Cut a large circle out of fairly stiff cardboard. Divide it into eight sections and glue a picture of a weather clue on each section. For example, your weather wheel might have a sun, a cloud, snow, rain, a lightning bolt, wind, something hot, and something cold. (You can cut pictures out of magazines, or draw them on construction paper and glue them down.)

Cut two pointers out of stiff cardboard and fasten them to the center of the dial with a big paper fastener.

Each morning take the children on a short weather walk to see how to set the weather wheel. Is it hot and clear? Rainy and windy? Snowy and cold?

After the wheel is set, hang it up so everyone can see it. If the weather changes during the day, take the wheel down and let one of the children reset it. After a few weeks of using the weather wheel, your group will be anxiously watching the weather as it changes.

Older children can make their own weather wheels on a smaller scale. They can cut circles out of cardboard, paste pictures down, and make pointers. Then they can take their weather wheels home to keep track of the weather on their own.

A Fold-Out Cloud Book

Make an accordion-style cloud book.

Objective:
Record and identify different types of clouds.

Ages:
Primary and Intermediate

Materials:
- *5 sheets of 8½ × 11" white or light blue paper for each person*
- *clear tape*
- *cardboard*
- *colored pencils, markers, and chalk*
- *magazines (for cutting pictures from)*
- *copies of the Cloud Chart insert*

Subjects:
Science and Art

Have your kids keep a record of the clouds they see and the information they find out about clouds by making their own cloud books. In the books they can include:

- notes from sky-watching for a week (or on and off through the year) and sketches of the clouds as they change from day to day
- descriptions of the sky at different times of the same day
- a cloud journal with daily entries about what is happening in the sky
- cloud poems (see page 23)
- a story about "A Day in the Life of Connie Cumulus" or some other cloud-related story
- cloud photographs cut from magazines
- a cloud chart (see the Cloud Chart insert)
- cloud vocabulary words such as *condense, evaporate, fog,* and so on
- a cloud mural

Here's how to make an easy accordion book that folds out and gives a lot of writing and drawing space:
1. Tape five sheets of paper together, side to side.
2. Tape a piece of 8½ × 11-inch cardboard to each end of the paper.
3. Fold the paper accordion-style, as shown. You can either use each page separately or unfold all the pages and draw a huge cloud mural on one whole side of the book.

Lightning on the Loose

I n the first part of this two-part activity, you can demonstrate how static electricity forms (which is how charges begin to separate and build in a cloud). And in the second part, your group can learn what to do and not to do in an electrical storm.

BALLOONS, PUFFED RICE, AND COMBS

The bolt of lightning you see streaking through the sky is electricity. And it all starts with the buildup of static electric charges inside storm clouds. Here are several ways to show your group how static electricity forms:

- Unwind a roll of cloth friction tape in a dark room. Ask your group what caused the sparks that result. (static electricity)
- Blow up two balloons and rub them on your sleeve. Then touch them together in a dark room. You should see sparks of static electricity.

- Run a comb through your hair and then put it into a bowl of dry puffed rice. Grains of rice will stick to the comb. After they lose their charge they will fall off.
- Shuffle across a carpet in a dark room, then touch a doorknob, radiator, or other metal object. You will see a spark jump from your finger to the metal object. (Ideas adapted from *Owlie Skywarn's Lightning Book* by Dr. Franklyn M. Branley and Leonard Kessler. See page 63 for how to order the *Owlie Skywarn* booklets.)

LOOK OUT FOR LIGHTNING

As a follow-up to these demonstrations, pass out page 35. Have the children mark a red X where they think lightning might strike. Then have them mark a blue X on the safest place for someone to be during a thunderstorm.

Afterward, discuss lightning safety and go over these lightning safety rules from the National Weather Service:

1. If you are outside and a thunderstorm develops, go into a house, large building, or enclosed car (not a convertible).
2. If you're stuck outside and can't make it to a building or car, remember to *stay away from:*
   - metal pipes, wire clotheslines, and metal fences
   - lakes, ponds, oceans, or any other body of water (If you are in the water, get out immediately and go to a shelter.)
   - tractors and all farm equipment
   - railroad tracks
   - sheds in open areas
   - bicycles, scooters, golf carts, and motorcycles
   - tall trees that stand alone in a field or yard
3. If you're in a forest, go to a low area where there are smaller trees. If the area is open, go to a ravine or valley but watch for flash floods.
4. If you're in a field or prairie and can't get to a building or car, crouch in a huddled position but don't lie down. (You want to make yourself as short as possible, but don't spread out on the wet ground.)
5. If you're in a building, don't use a phone unless there is an emergency. Also stay away from electrical appliances and plumbing.

LITTLE-KNOWN LIGHTNING FACTS

- Lightning strikes the earth about 100 times each second.
- A flash of lightning can sometimes be over 5 miles (8 km) long.
- Lightning temperatures can sometimes reach over 50,000° F (28,000° C)—that's over five times hotter than the sun's surface!
- More people are killed by lightning each year than by hurricanes, blizzards, or tornadoes.
- On the average, more than 100 people are electrocuted by lightning in the United States each year.
- By counting the seconds between a lightning flash and the thunder that follows, you can estimate the distance between you and the lightning: about every five seconds equals one mile.

Snow in a Box

Make a cloud in a box and watch it snow.

Objective:
Observe and describe the conditions that cause snow to form.

Ages:
Intermediate and Advanced

Materials:
- *dry ice (about 40 pounds [18 kg])*
- *thick gloves*
- *powerful flashlight or slide projector*
- *hammer*
- *towel*
- *newspaper*
- *two boxes, one a little smaller than the other. The larger box should be about 36 × 48" and the smaller box should be about 12 × 24".*
- *black construction paper*
- *thermometer*

Subject:
Science

In this activity you can make your own snow-forming cloud in a box and show your group what it takes to make snow. First explain that in order for snow to form there need to be:

- a cloud that is supercooled (The water droplets are below freezing.)
- particles of ice for water vapor to condense on
- cold air and ground temperatures so the snow doesn't melt as it falls

Then show your group that you can create these conditions in a special dry-ice box. Here's how to do it:

1. Line the inside of the smaller box with black construction paper.
2. Put the smaller box inside the larger box and fill the space between them with small chunks of dry ice. (Always handle dry ice with gloves. It is so cold that it can stick to your skin and cause frostbite.) Put newspaper over the top layer of dry ice to keep it from evaporating.
3. Cover the smaller box and allow the air inside it to drop to freezing temperatures. This will take about eight to ten minutes.
4. Now you're ready to make snow. Let a small group of children gather around the box to observe. (If too many kids gather around, it will be hard for everyone to see.) Warn them not to touch the dry ice.

(continued on next page)

5. Remove the cover and breathe into the box to fill it with water vapor. This will form a cloud that floats in the air of the smaller box. (The vapor from your breath is warm. As it cools, some of it condenses, forming a cloud.) Have the kids watch the cloud for a moment. It's a great way for them to see how clouds move. (They flow, almost like water.)

6. Hammer a small piece of dry ice into very tiny bits. (Put the ice in a towel to smash it.)

7. Turn off the lights and use a powerful flashlight or the light from a slide projector and shine it in at an angle through the cloud.

8. Drop a few of the tiny pieces of dry ice through the cloud. You will see snowflakes form in the cloud and fall on the black paper. The crystals "sparkle" because light reflects off their flat surfaces. (You won't get a lot of snow, but this demonstration will show kids how snowflakes form.) Discuss what happens. (See the background information on page 26.)

As a follow-up, you might want to have the kids make their own snowflakes out of soda straws (see page 59). Also see "Snowflake Bentley," *Ranger Rick,* December 1982, pp. 34–37 for more about snow and snowflake activities.

Weather Wizards

Play a team match-up game about different kinds of weather.

Objective:
Discuss two weather-related characteristics for each of the following: a sunny day, a tornado, a blizzard, and a hurricane.

Ages:
Intermediate and Advanced

Materials:
- *pictures of a sunny day, a hurricane, a tornado, and a blizzard*
- *construction paper*
- *index cards*
- *glue*
- *magazines*

Subject:
Science

What kind of weather is taking place when cloud droplets grow bigger and clump together, electrical charges build up in the clouds and on the ground, hot air expands quickly, and the air pressure drops? If you guessed a thunderstorm, you're right. In this activity your group can make their own deductions about the weather. It's a good way to challenge them to think while reviewing weather facts.

Before the activity, write each of these weather clues on a separate index card, but don't write down the type of weather it represents:

A SUNNY DAY

Clues:
- low humidity
- barometer probably steady or rising
- anti-cyclone
- small cumulus clouds here and there in the sky
- the sunset the night before was a deep pink color
- usually a high pressure system

HURRICANE

Clues:
- Andy, Betty, Cesar, Diana, Ed, Fran, and Gustav
- eye
- born in a hot, moist air mass over the ocean
- wind speeds of over 74 miles (117 km) per hour
- huge storm surges
- cyclones and typhoons
- would probably never happen in Ohio

BLIZZARD

Clues:
- can't see the clouds
- bitterly cold winds, usually from the north
- most severe ones occur in central Canada, parts of Russia, and the Great Plains of the United States
- plates, columns, and needles pile up
- symbol on a weather map: ✳✳✳
- visibility can approach zero
- drifting and blowing

TORNADO

Clues:
- usually lasts only a few minutes
- best to stay in basement or cellar
- most violent of all storms
- very sudden pressure drop
- majority occur in central United States from the Gulf Coast to the Northern Plains
- cumulonimbus clouds
- funnel clouds

(continued on page 33)

SOME COMMON CLOUDS

LOW CLOUDS (form from ground level to 5000 feet [1500 m]):

- *Fog*—A cloud in contact with the ground. Occurs frequently on clear nights in low-lying areas and near bodies of water.

- *Cumulus*—Puffy, white clouds that bulge out at their tops like cauliflower. Cumulus clouds mean good weather when there's a lot of space between the clouds and they don't build up very much.

- *Stratus*—Unbroken sheets of low, gray clouds. Bring light rain, light snow, or drizzle.

- *Stratocumulus*—Look like cumulus clouds pressed together in layers. Gray and white patches make them resemble dirty cotton balls. Rain or snow might be on the way if they grow darker.

- *Nimbostratus*—A thicker layer of clouds than stratus. Nimbostratus clouds completely block out the sun and steady rain or snow falls from them.

- *Cumulonimbus*—Starting as *low* cumulus clouds, cumulonimbus clouds can grow into dark, towering mountains that reach up to 60,000 feet (18,000 m) in severe thunderstorms. Also known as "thunderheads," their tops often flatten into an anvil shape. Winds blow violently up and down in the clouds, causing heavy rain, thunder, and lightning. (Often classified as vertical clouds because they can reach from low to high elevations.)

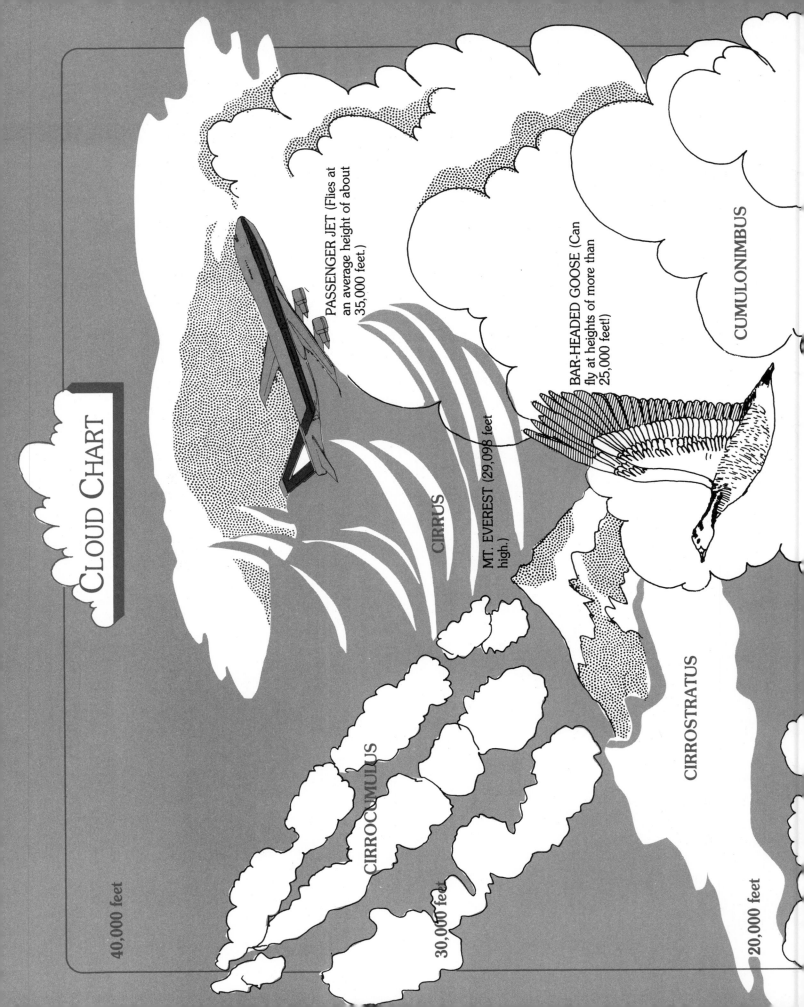

Cloud Chart

40,000 feet

PASSENGER JET (Flies at an average height of about 35,000 feet.)

CIRRUS

MT. EVEREST (29,098 feet high.)

BAR-HEADED GOOSE (Can fly at heights of more than 25,000 feet!)

CUMULONIMBUS

CIRROCUMULUS

30,000 feet

CIRROSTRATUS

20,000 feet

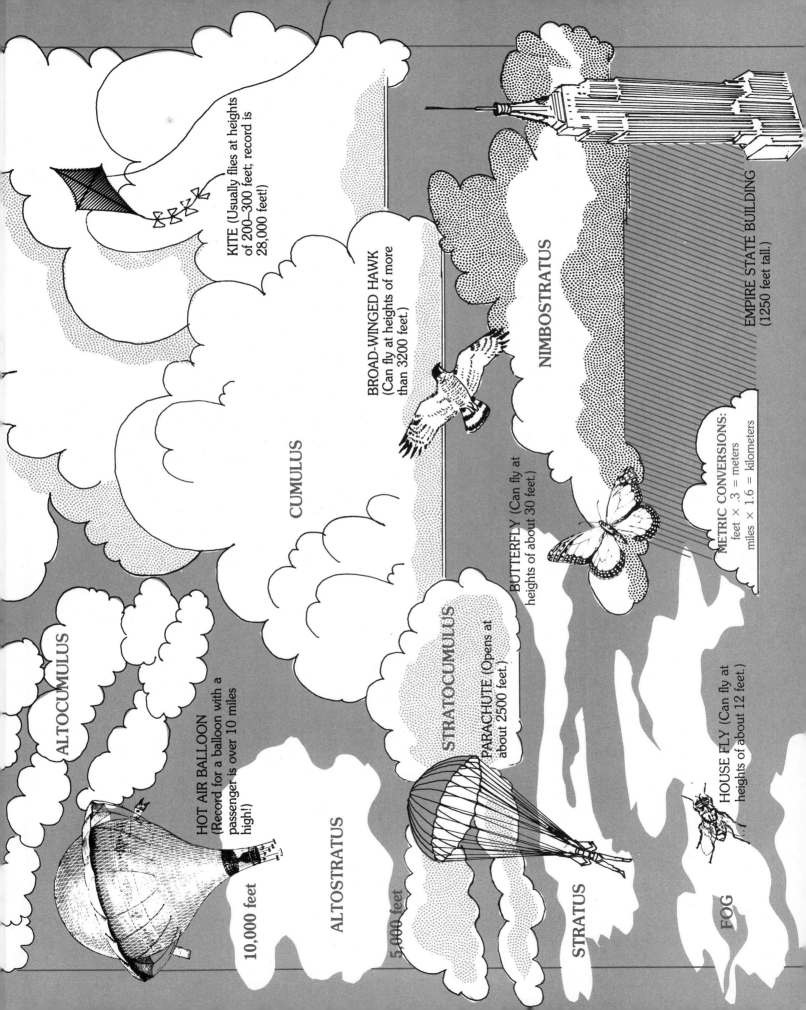

KITE (Usually flies at heights of 200–300 feet; record is 28,000 feet!)

BROAD-WINGED HAWK (Can fly at heights of more than 3200 feet.)

CUMULUS

NIMBOSTRATUS

EMPIRE STATE BUILDING (1250 feet tall.)

METRIC CONVERSIONS:
feet × .3 = meters
miles × 1.6 = kilometers

BUTTERFLY (Can fly at heights of about 30 feet.)

ALTOCUMULUS

HOT AIR BALLOON (Record for a balloon with a passenger is over 10 miles high!)

10,000 feet

ALTOSTRATUS

5,000 feet

STRATOCUMULUS

PARACHUTE (Opens at about 2500 feet.)

HOUSE FLY (Can fly at heights of about 12 feet.)

STRATUS

FOG

MIDDLE CLOUDS (form from 6000 to 20,000 feet [1800 to 6000 m]):

- *Altocumulus*—Rows of small white and gray rolls, or scattered white and gray puffs of different shapes. Some altocumulus clouds look like towers or turrets.
- *Altostratus*—Grayish layers of clouds that make the sun or moon look as if they're behind frosted glass. If they thicken, expect rain or snow.

HIGH CLOUDS (form from 20,000 to 40,000 feet [6000 to 12,000 m]):

- *Cirrus*—Often called "mares' tails," these wispy, white clouds form higher than most other clouds. They are the first sign of an approaching warm front and can mean rain or snow is on the way.
- *Cirrocumulus*—Thin, white rolls of clouds (much smaller than altocumulus clouds) that look like ripples in the sand or scales on a fish. (A sky full of cirrocumulus clouds is often called a "mackerel sky.") These clouds often indicate that a warm front is on the way.
- *Cirrostratus*—A thin layer of cirrus clouds that forms a hazy circle or halo around the sun or moon. (The ice crystals in the clouds act as prisms, scattering white light into a spectrum.)

Next cut out a picture of a hurricane, a tornado, a blizzard, and a sunny day from magazines. (If you can't find photographs, draw your own pictures.) Glue each picture to a piece of construction paper and hang each in a different spot in the room. (You can also do this activity outside. Just hang the pictures on trees or posts in a field or grassy area.)

Now explain to the kids that they are going to play a weather game. Each person will get to pick a weather clue out of a hat. All of the clues are different and each one fits one of the four types of weather shown in the pictures—a blizzard, a sunny day, a hurricane, or a tornado. For example, a clue reading "plates, columns, and needles pile up" would fit with the picture of the blizzard because it describes characteristic shapes of snowflakes.

Explain that there are two objects to the game. The first is to decide which of the four weather pictures your clue best fits. The second is to find the rest of the kids who have clues that fit the same picture that your clue does and line up as a complete team under the appropriate weather picture. Explain that no one will know which team anybody else is on until the kids start mingling and comparing clues. (There should be about the same number of clues per team, but it can vary, depending on the size of your group.)

Here's how to play:

1. Have each person draw a clue out of a hat. Tell the kids to read their clues silently and decide which of the four weather pictures the clues fit best.

2. Tell the group how many members there are in each of the four teams so they know how many it will take to complete a team. Try to make the teams as even as possible. (For example, there might be six clues for a sunny day, seven clues for hurricane, seven clues for tornado, and six clues for blizzard. So to win, the hurricane team must find all seven of its members. Explain that some teams have more members because some of the clues for those teams may be a little easier.)

3. Then let the kids mill around and try to find other members of their teams. Since some clues are easier than others, "core groups" will form that know they belong together. But other clues will be less definite. Have the "core kids" work together to find the other members of their teams. Encourage the kids to discuss the clues.

4. Only when all the members of a team find each other can they line up under their weather picture. The first group to line up wins and becomes the official *Weather Wizards!*

5. After all the teams finish, have the kids read their clues to the group, one at a time. Discuss why each clue "belongs" to a certain type of weather.

Can you guess the riddles? (We've given you the first one.)

1. Warm air rising up so high
   Cools, condenses, and
   makes me "fly."

   <u>C</u>   <u>L</u>   <u>O</u>   <u>U</u>   <u>D</u>

2. You cannot see me with
   your eyes,
   But I make trees move when
   I go by.

   _ _ _ _

3. We have six sides and many
   brothers,
   But each one's different from
   all the others.

   _ _ _ _ _ _ _ _ _

4. I fall to earth and then I
   freeze,
   Coating pavement, fields,
   and trees.

   _ _ _ _ _

5. A million amps of
   electricity—
   You don't want to get hit by
   me!

   _ _ _ _ _ _ _ _ _

6. Layers of ice freeze till I fall,
   Small as a pea or big as a
   ball.

   _ _ _ _

7. Lightning heats the air so
   fast
   That you can hear my
   mighty blast.

   _ _ _ _ _ _ _

8. My eye is calm, but just
   watch out
   My winds mean
   trouble—there's no doubt!

   _ _ _ _ _ _ _ _ _ _

9. Two hundred miles an hour
   I whirl,
   Causing great damage
   wherever I twirl!

   _ _ _ _ _ _ _

10. Up in the North is where I
    prowl,
    With blinding snow and
    winds that howl.

    _ _ _ _ _ _ _ _

11. Most clouds form up high in
    the sky,
    But down near the ground is
    where I lie.

    _ _ _

RANGER RICK'S NATURESCOPE: WILD ABOUT WEATHER

RANGER RICK'S NATURESCOPE: WILD ABOUT WEATHER

THE WEATHER WATCHERS

The chair creaks, your hair gets frizzy, the chickens are restless, and the flies bite more. The cows scratch, the dogs sniff the air, and the honey bees are huddled in the hive. According to weather folklore, these happenings all point to one thing—rain! Even though some of them are based on fact, it's probably not a good idea to depend on any for a reliable forecast.

Weather Watchers of the Past: The first book of popular weather forecasting was written in 300 B.C., when one of Aristotle's favorite students, Theophrastus, published *The Book of Signs*. In it he listed over 200 rules for predicting the weather. Many of his sayings have been translated into ones we still hear today. And other sayings have been created since then by farmers, hunters, anglers, sailors, and other people who needed to spend a lot of time outside.

You'll find that weather sayings about clouds, wind direction, the appearance of the sky, and the condition of the atmosphere are the most reliable. But ones that are based on plants and animals are less reliable in making an accurate forecast. And those based on the moon and planets seem to have no scientific basis at all.

Meteorologists Move In: Instead of relying on folklore for our weather forecasting, we now rely on the science of *meteorology* (the study of the atmosphere). *Meteorologists* are scientists trained in physics, mathematics, chemistry, and computer science. They use their training, skill, and experience not only to forecast the weather but also to study how the atmosphere functions and changes, how people affect weather, and how weather affects people.

Most weather forecasts that you see on TV, hear on the radio, or read in the newspaper are based on data and observations issued by the National Weather Service (NWS). With over 300 offices across the country, the NWS employs more meteorologists than any other government agency. (The NWS is part of NOAA—the National Oceanic and Atmospheric Administration.)

Many other meteorologists conduct research for other branches of NOAA as well as for the military, the space program, state and federal agencies, and universities where they also teach. And many meteorologists also work for private industry and private weather companies. Many TV weather presenters are trained meteorologists too.

"And Tomorrow's Weather Will Be . . .": Thousands of people all over the world help to gather the weather information that is needed to make predictions. Facts and figures pour into the National Meteorological Center in Washington, D.C., around the clock, coming from weather stations on ships, on balloons, on airport decks, on university campuses, and other places all over the world. Every 12 hours this information is fed into giant computers and transformed into accurate, up-to-date weather maps. A meteorologist takes all the data and uses his or her skills and experience to come up with a reliable forecast.

Tools of the Meteorology Trade: Meteorologists have been using weather instruments for hundreds of years to measure and record temperature, air pressure, precipitation, humidity, and wind direction and speed. Here are some of the "old standbys" and what they do:

- thermometer: measures air temperature
- barometer: measures air pressure

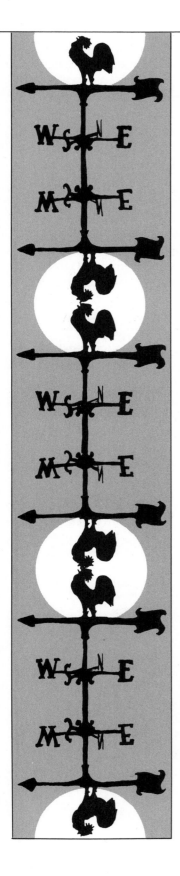

- rain gauge: measures rainfall
- snowstick: measures snowfall
- psychrometer: measures relative humidity
- hygrometer: measures humidity
- wind vane and wind sock: measure wind direction
- anemometer: measures wind speed

Within the last fifty years, meteorologists have used weather balloons, satellites, radar, and computers to improve the accuracy of their forecasts. Here's how they work:

- **Weather Balloons** carry instruments that measure temperature, pressure, and humidity at different altitudes in the atmosphere. Special recording equipment in the balloons converts readings from these instruments into electrical impulses and transmits the impulses to earth. The balloons are tracked with radar to find wind speed and direction.
- **Weather Satellites** send back information about storms, fronts, cloud cover, geographical features of the earth, and air and ocean temperatures. Each satellite is equipped with light and heat sensors, recorders, a radio receiver and transmitter, and other recording instruments.

  The first weather satellite, TIROS I, was launched in 1960. Since then it has been replaced with newer, more sophisticated satellites. Today there are several satellites sending back data. Some of these satellites orbit the earth several times a day; others remain fixed over a single area. The satellite pictures you see on TV weather reports are from GOES satellites, which are located at altitudes of about 22,500 miles (36,000 km).
- **Radar** sends out radio waves at the speed of light. These waves bounce off raindrops, snow, or hail inside a cloud and reflect energy back to a radar antenna, which usually looks like a huge dish sitting on its side. The radar receiver picks up the radio waves and changes them into dots and blips of light that show up on a fluorescent screen. When the weather forecaster on TV shows you the "radar picture," he or she is showing you the picture of what the radar pulses reflected off—precipitation-sized particles, mountains, and other obstacles (but not clouds). One of the "tricks" to being a good meteorologist is learning how to "read" and interpret the radar. (Radar stands for **RA**dio **D**etection **A**nd **R**ange.)
- **Computers** can do millions of operations per second, figuring out math equations that relate to the movements of fronts, air pressure systems, and storms. Computers also help meteorologists build numerical weather models that can predict future weather patterns. As computers become more sophisticated, so does weather forecasting.

Mapping the Weather: Computers take all the information from weather stations, satellites, and weather balloons and convert it into two kinds of weather maps: surface maps and upper air maps.

Surface Maps show what the weather was like on the surface of the earth at the time the observations were made. (See page 41 for information about reading surface maps.) *Upper Air Maps* help give meteorologists clues about how the weather will likely change by recording conditions high in the atmosphere.

Make a Simple Weather Watcher

Record changes in humidity using special test paper.

Objective:
Define humidity and demonstrate how it changes from day to day.

Ages:
Primary and Intermediate

Materials:
- **cobalt chloride test paper (see end of activity for how to order)**
- **cardboard**
- **glue**
- **crayons or markers**
- **string or yarn**
- **construction paper**
- **scissors**
- **tape**

Subject:
Science

To introduce young kids to weather forecasting, have them make their own "magic" weather watchers. First have each person draw and cut out a weather picture using cardboard, crayons, markers, construction paper, scissors, and other art supplies. (Umbrellas, satellites, suns, rainbows, clouds, snowpeople, and animals are good subjects to suggest.)

Next pass out strips of cobalt chloride paper and have the kids tape one or two strips of it to their weather pictures. (Tell them to tape only a small corner of each strip down and let the rest hang freely. Caution them not to put the strips in their mouths or get the strips wet.)

Finally, poke a hole in the top of each picture using a pencil, and tie a piece of string or yarn to the top so the kids can hang their weather watchers.

Then tell everyone to take his or her weather watcher home, hang it in a protected place outside, and watch the special strips of paper every day. What happens? (Cobalt chloride paper changes color as the humidity changes. When there is less water in the air it becomes blue. When there is more water in the air it becomes pink. Many times humid air is a sign of rainy weather and dry air is a sign of fair weather.)

Ask the kids if they can think of any other ways to tell if there is a lot of water in the air. (High humidity makes you feel sticky and wet and also makes some people's hair get frizzy.)

Have the group experiment with their weather watchers. They can take them into their bathrooms when they take a bath, into their basements, and into their attics. They can also put them in their refrigerators.

Have the kids keep a record of what color the strips become in each location. (It should be hot and humid in a closed-up bathroom when someone is taking a bath or shower. Some basements are damp and some attics are dry. And the air in a refrigerator should be fairly dry.)

To order cobalt chloride test paper write to Carolina Biological Supply Company, Burlington, NC 27215, and request Cobalt Chloride Qualitative Test Paper #89-5570. Or call (800) 334-5551.

Feathered and Furry Forecasters

Discuss weather folklore and take a weather folklore quiz.

Objective:
Discuss how animals have been used in folklore to predict the weather.

Ages:
Primary, Intermediate, and Advanced

Materials:
- **copies of page 44**

Subjects:
Science and Folklore

In this activity your kids can take a look at some common weather folklore about animals. First pass out copies of page 44 and give the kids time to decide whether each saying is true or false. Then read through each of the sayings on the page. For each saying, ask the kids how many of them think the saying is true. After you've tallied the responses, explain that all the sayings on the list are false. Then talk about weather folklore in general, explaining that a lot of sayings that focus on animals are true only part of the time or not true at all. And even though scientists think that some animals react to changes in air pressure or wind direction, they don't think animals can reliably "predict" weather patterns.

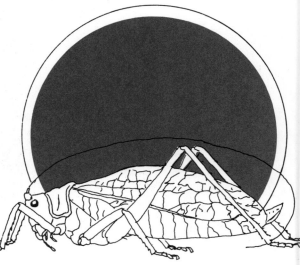

On the other hand, some of the weather folklore that is based on clouds, wind direction, or the appearance of the sky is fairly reliable and can often help predict the weather. For example, the following rhyme has a lot of truth to it:

When the clouds appear like rocks and towers,

The earth's refreshed by frequent showers.

The "rocks and towers" describe what happens to cumulus clouds before a storm. As they pile up and begin to tower in the sky, they become cumulonimbus clouds, which bring thunderstorms and rain.

Say It with Symbols

Use weather symbols to create a story.

Objectives:
Draw five weather symbols and explain what they mean. Use weather symbols to create a story.

Ages:
Intermediate

Materials:
- *copies of page 45*
- *easel paper*
- *glue or paste*
- *markers and crayons*

Subjects:
Science and Creative Writing

Special symbols and codes on weather maps explain the type of clouds, how much of the sky is covered by clouds, the type of precipitation that's falling, the temperature, the wind speed, the wind direction, and other important weather data. The symbols are used because they take up a lot less space than words.

Official weather maps use an international code system so meteorologists around the world can read and understand the weather maps from other countries. This system uses over 100 different symbols and number codes.

Most of us see only a few of these official symbols because weather maps for TV and newspapers are often simplified. And sometimes TV and newspaper weather reporters will change the official symbols to make them easier for everyone to understand. For example, you might see snow symbolized as *** or Ⓢ on TV. And rain might be •• or \\\\. Unfortunately use of nonstandard symbols may confuse more than it simplifies.

In this activity your kids will get a chance to learn some of the symbols that are used by meteorologists and then use the symbols to write their own weather stories.

Give each person a copy of page 45, a large piece of easel paper, and some markers or crayons. Explain that everyone is going to make up a weather story using at least eight of the symbols from the Copycat Page you handed out. For example, the first part of a story might look like this: *Today was the big day. But when I got up in the morning it was* ● *. I sure hoped it wouldn't* •• *today because that could really ruin the big camping trip. I looked at the barometer and saw that it was* \ *. "I'd better bring a raincoat," I said to myself.*

The children can paste down their weather symbols or they can just draw the symbols with markers. When everyone is done, give each person a chance to read his or her story to the rest of the group. Then hang the finished stories up for everyone else to read.

Fishy Forecasts

Catch the mistakes in ten phony weather forecasts.

Objectives:
Describe a weather forecast. Identify errors in faulty forecasts.

Ages:
Intermediate and Advanced

Materials:
- *copies of page 46*
- *lined paper*
- *pencils or pens*

Subject:
Science

Suppose you heard a weather forecast that went something like this: *Snow developing this morning, accumulating 6 to 8 inches before tapering off tonight. Currently it's 32° F outside under clear skies. Relative humidity is 93% and the barometer is on the rise.*

If you were "up" on your weather facts you might think this particular forecast was a little odd. An approaching storm usually means a falling—not rising—barometer, and thickening clouds—not a clear sky.

For this activity, we've fabricated 10 weather forecasts. Three of them make sense, but the rest have parts that don't. It's up to your group to decide which forecasts "work" and which don't. Here's what to do:

First pass out a copy of page 46 to each person (see right-hand column for answers to this Copycat Page) and a sheet of lined paper. You can have the kids work alone or in small groups to evaluate each forecast. (If you're just starting a weather unit and the kids aren't familiar with weather conditions and forecasts, this can be a good research activity.)

Have each person make an answer sheet by numbering from 1 to 10 on the sheet of lined paper. (Tell them to leave two or three lines after each number.) Now have them write on their answer sheets whether they think each forecast is "OK" or "Not OK." For example, if they decide the first forecast is a good one, they should write "OK" by number 1 on their answer sheets. If they think the forecast doesn't make sense, they should write "Not OK," along with a few words that explain what is wrong with it.

After everyone is done, lead a discussion about the forecasts. You can also have the kids work in teams of four or five to come up with their own "good" and "bad" forecasts. Then each team can try to stump the others by reading one of their forecasts and having the rest of the teams decide whether it makes sense. The forecasting team gets a point each time another team makes an incorrect judgment.

Here's an explanation of the forecasts on page 46:

1. OK. High pressure systems usually mean fair weather.
2. Not OK. It would be impossible for rain—especially a heavy downpour—to fall from a clear sky.
3. Not OK. Temperatures must be below freezing and skies must be clear for frost to form. Also there would not be a 40% chance of precipitation with frost.
4. Not OK. The relative humidity is always higher than 3% with or without a storm. But it would be higher than usual with a storm approaching.
5. OK. Hot days and high humidity without thunderstorms are typical of heat wave weather.
6. Not OK. If snow fell all night, the chance of precipitation would not decrease to 30% before midnight.
7. Not OK. Sleet and hail develop in two different ways and one cannot change into the other. The forecast is also invalid for another reason: Thunderheads, in which hailstones form, don't normally develop in cold winter air.
8. Not OK. Low pressure systems often bring, not take away, strong winds. And winds are often from the northwest *after* a Low passes, not before.
9. Not OK. A high pressure system usually means fair weather.
10. OK. An approaching snowstorm usually means a drop in pressure.

First with the Forecast

Play a weather map game.

Objective:
Use weather symbols to interpret a simplified weather map.

Ages:
Intermediate and Advanced

Materials:
- *copies of pages 45 and 47*
- *small bell for each team*

Subjects:
Geography and Science

nce your kids become weather symbol experts, show them how the symbols are organized on a National Weather Service (NWS) map. (You might be able to get copies of old weather maps by contacting your local NWS office, a local university, or a TV weather station.) Explain that official weather offices across the country send data to the National Weather Service on cloud cover, precipitation, air pressure, visibility, wind speed, wind direction, and cloud type. All these data are represented on the national map by *station models*. A station model shows where the weather station is located and has all the weather data surrounding it. Here's an example of how a station model might look for the Ohio Valley in winter:

SAMPLE STATION MODEL

Wind speed (18–22 miles per hour)
High cloud type (cirrus)
Middle cloud type (altocumulus)
Barometric pressure at sea level (1024.7 millibars)
Wind direction (from the northwest)
Temperature (in degrees Fahrenheit) → 31
Amount of barometric change in past 3 hours (in tenths of millibars)
247
Visibility (¾ of a mile) → ¾ ✳✳
+28
Barometer tendency in past 3 hours (rising)
Present weather (continuous light snow)
30
Weather in past 6 hours (rain)
.45
Dew point (in degrees Fahrenheit)
Low cloud type (fractostratus)
Amount of precipitation in last 6 hours
Total amount of clouds (sky completely covered)

Each number and symbol represents a certain bit of data. (The position of each number and symbol is always the same, except for the wind direction symbol which points to the direction the wind is coming from.)

As meteorologists study the station models on surface weather maps, they connect areas of equal pressure with lines called isobars. (The isobars are similar to contour lines on a topographical map that connect areas of equal altitude.) The patterns of isobars show areas of low and

high pressure and allow forecasters to see how air pressure, wind speed, and wind direction are related. (Isobars that are close together show that pressure change is rapid and that the winds are blowing fast. When isobars are far apart, the winds are slower.)

Isobars also point out pressure systems. If pressure increases toward the center of an area, it is labeled H for High; if pressure decreases, it is labeled L for Low. (Some newspaper weather maps have isobars drawn in.)

Pass out copies of page 45 and tell your kids that they are going to play a weather game in which they will need to know these symbols. Explain that these are just a few of the symbols used by the National Weather Service. Then draw a sample station model on the board so they can see how the cloud cover symbol ○ is connected to the wind speed and wind direction symbols. The rest of the weather data surrounds the cloud cover circle. Explain that the circle for cloud cover also indicates the location of the weather station where the readings were taken.

Tell the kids they will need to brush up on the locations of cities, states, and provinces in the United States and Canada to play the game. When they're ready to play, pass out copies of the map on page 47. Divide the group into four or five teams and give each team a small bell. Explain that you'll be asking several questions about the map (see the list at the end of this activity). Give the kids a few minutes to study the map before you start.

Now assign one person in each team to be the team's speaker. Tell the kids that when you ask a question they must quietly discuss the answer as a team. When a team has agreed on an answer, the speaker can ring the team's bell. The first speaker to "ring" gets the chance to answer the question for his or her team. (To give everyone a chance to speak up, change the speakers after every question or two.) A correct answer wins 10 points for the team. But a wrong answer means the team loses 5 points. The team with the most points at the end of the game wins.

(continued on next page)

1. Is the barometer rising, falling, or steady in Richmond, Virginia? (rising)
2. Name the states where it is snowing. (Utah, Wyoming, Montana, Colorado, North Dakota, and Alaska)
3. Name the provinces where it is snowing. (Saskatchewan and Manitoba)
4. What's the wind direction in Las Vegas, Nevada? (northwest)
5. In which state(s) is it drizzling? (Texas)
6. Which one of the following cities is having a rainstorm: Phoenix, Arizona; Las Vegas, Nevada; or Minneapolis, Minnesota? (Minneapolis)
7. Which states have cumulus clouds in the sky? (New York and Pennsylvania)
8. A warm front is passing through which states and provinces? (Kansas, Nebraska, Colorado, and Missouri)
9. Name a city that is covered with fog. (San Francisco)
10. Where is the center of a high pressure system? (between Ontario and Quebec)
11. What is the sky cover over Montreal? (partly cloudy)
12. Over which city can you see cirrus clouds: Kansas City, Missouri, or Tulsa, Oklahoma? (Tulsa)
13. What kind of storm might soon hit New Orleans, Louisiana? (hurricane)
14. What is the sky cover in the Northwest Territories? (clear)
15. What are the wind direction and cloud cover in Pierre, South Dakota? (east and cloudy)
16. Is the barometer rising or falling over the Grand Canyon? (rising)

Weather by the Chart

Use a weather chart to make a forecast.

Objective:
Explain how cloud types, wind direction, and pressure can be used to forecast the weather.

Ages:
Intermediate and Advanced

Materials:
- *barometer*
- *wind sock*
- *copies of page 48*
- *copies of the Cloud Chart insert*
- *heavy construction paper or cardboard*

Subjects:
Science and Math

eather forecasting isn't easy. You need to know how clouds, wind, pressure, and temperature all interact before you can figure out what kind of weather is coming.

In this activity your group can practice forecasting by using a simple weather forecasting chart (page 48) that focuses on cloud types, pressure, and wind direction.

For help with identifying clouds, pass out copies of the Cloud Chart insert. (You can also send away for a full-color poster that has photographs of the different kinds of clouds. To order, see page 64 in the Appendix.)

For directions on how to make a wind sock, see page 60. If possible, use a mercury or aneroid barometer for the air pressure readings. (Homemade barometers usually aren't accurate.)

Here's how to use the weather forecasting chart:

Divide the group into three teams: the Cloud Team, the Pressure Team, and the Wind Team. Then, at a specific time each day, have each of the weather forecast teams take a "reading" on what's happening outside. (The Pressure Team will have had to have taken one or two readings earlier in the day to find out if the pressure is rising, falling, or staying the same.) Then have the teams compare their readings to the lists on page 48. For example, if there are cumulus clouds outside, the Cloud Team should find the word *cumulus* on the cloud list. Then have them write down the number that corresponds to the cloud type. (In the case of cumulus clouds, the number would be 7.)

Have the Pressure and Wind Teams take readings with their instruments and do the same thing. Then have the teams add the three numbers to get a forecast number. By looking at the forecasting chart they can find the forecast that matches their number.

(The Weather Chart was reprinted, with permission, from *A Guide to Weather Watching* by Marty Silver, 1981. See page 64 for ordering information.)

FORECASTING FOLLOW-UPS

- Keep a large chart that records how accurately the forecasting chart works. You can list the date and then draw a smiling face 😊 if the forecast was correct, a sad face 😞 if the forecast was incorrect, and a no-expression face 😐 if it was partly correct.
- Discuss why a general forecasting chart like this probably won't work all the time and in all areas of the country. (Many areas are influenced by local geography, such as mountains, valleys, lakes, deserts, and oceans. Some areas are more influenced by the jet stream, which might bring different winds and weather patterns to an area.)
- Have each team keep a weather notebook and record their observations every day. If they do this activity throughout the entire year, the kids will be able to watch how clouds, wind direction, and pressure sometimes change with the seasons.
- Have the kids bring in newspaper weather maps for a week, paste them down in a notebook, and notice how weather patterns move across the country. Discuss how weather system movements can affect their own forecasts.

BRANCHING OUT: MATH

- Continue this forecasting activity over several weeks or months so you can calculate how accurate the forecasting chart is. For example, if the forecast was correct two times during a four-day period, it was only 50% accurate. If it was accurate 24 days out of 26 days, then it was 92% accurate.
- Have your group compare their forecasts to those of the weather forecasters from TV, radio, or newspapers. Have each team watch or listen to a different station and copy down the weather report from the evening news. Make a chart using construction paper or heavy cardboard and list the stations, their weather forecasters, and the face symbol that best represents the forecasts they gave.

  Again calculate the percentages to find out which forecaster was the most accurate. Then look at the accuracy of your forecasts. Are any of the teams better forecasters than the professionals?

Note: The *WeatherCycler,* listed on page 64 in the Appendix, is another good weather forecaster. And unlike some of the others, it lets you see *why* the forecast is what it is. (Advanced)

Forecasting Records	Sun	Mon	Tue	Wed	Thu	Fri	Sat
Our Forecast	🙂	😠	😐	😐			
Channel 4 Bud Front	😠	🙂	🙂	🙂			
Channel 7 Sally Waters	🙂	🙂	😠	😐			
Channel 12 Andy Swirl	😐	😐	🙂	🙂			

Which of these sayings are true and which are false? Mark your answers in the blanks.

1. When a cow bellows three times without stopping,
   A storm will come hopping.

   MOO
   MOOOO
   MMOOOO

   True _____   False _____

2. When you see a beaver carrying sticks in its mouth,
   It will be a hard winter—you'd better go south.

   True _____   False _____

   COCK-A-DOODLE-DOOOOOOOO

3. When the rooster crows at night,
   He tells you that a rain's in sight.

   True _____   False _____

4. When ants travel in a straight line, expect rain; when they scatter, expect fair weather.

   True _____   False _____

5. When squirrels lay in a big store of nuts, look for a hard winter.

   True _____

   False _____

   FEBRUARY
   1 2 3 4 5 6 7
   8 9 10 11 12 13 14
   15 16 17 18 19 20 21
   22 23 24 25 26 27 28

6. If the groundhog sees its shadow on Groundhog Day, there will be six more weeks of winter.

   True _____

   False _____

   NOVEMBER
   1 2 3 4 5
   7 8 9 10 11 12
   14 15 16 17 18 19
   21 22 23 24 25 26
   28 29 30 31

7. If a turkey's feathers are unusually thick by Thanksgiving, look for a hard winter.

   True _____   False _____

8. The wider the black bands on a woolly bear caterpillar, the colder the winter will be.

   True _____   False _____

Cirrus Clouds	Fog	Moderate Rain	Cloudy
Heavy Snow	Cumulus Clouds	Cold Front	Showers
Partly Cloudy	Thunderstorm	Low Pressure System	Drizzle
Cumulonimbus Clouds	Warm Front	Clear Skies	Barometer Steady
Hurricane	High Pressure System	Barometer Rising	Barometer Falling

Some of these forecasts make sense and others don't. Can you decide which ones are OK?

1. Cloudy with light rain this morning, but clearing this afternoon as a high pressure system approaches. Fair tonight and tomorrow. Chance of rain 60% this morning, decreasing to 10% tonight.

2. Clear and cool today; highs in the 50s. Remaining clear through tonight, with scattered showers and strong possibility of some heavy downpours. Lows in the low 40s.

3. Today, fair and cool, with highs in the 50s. Cloudy tonight, with lows in the low 40s and frost developing toward morning. Chance of precipitation is 40% today and tonight.

4. Severe thunderstorm watch in effect. Hot this afternoon, with temperatures in the low 90s. Barometric pressure 29.96 inches and falling; relative humidity 3%.

5. Heat wave continuing. Hot and humid with clear skies. High today near 100. Low tonight near 80.

6. Snow this afternoon and tonight, accumulating 8 to 10 inches before ending early tomorrow morning. Chance of precipitation 100% today, decreasing to 30% before midnight.

7. Winter storm watch this evening. Sleet developing, changing to hail before ending tonight. Lows in the low 30s.

8. Strong northwest winds today, diminishing as a low pressure system advances. Temperatures in the 50s this afternoon; falling into the mid 40s tonight.

9. Fair today, but increasing cloudiness tonight as a high pressure system moves into the area. Chance of rain 20% today, increasing to 90% tonight.

10. Partly cloudy today, with highs in the mid 30s. This evening, turning colder, with snow developing before midnight. Barometric pressure 29.80 inches and falling.

COPYCAT PAGE

FIRST WITH THE FORECAST

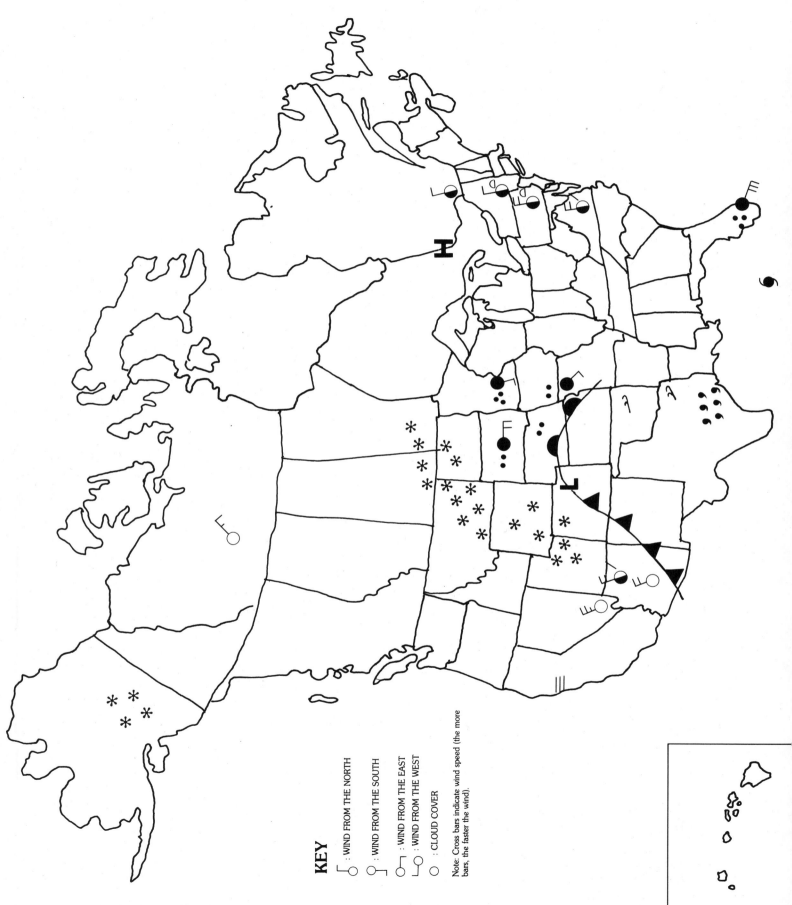

KEY

⌐₀ : WIND FROM THE NORTH

◯⌐ : WIND FROM THE SOUTH

⌐─◯ : WIND FROM THE EAST

└─◯ : WIND FROM THE WEST

◯ : CLOUD COVER

Note: Cross bars indicate wind speed (the more bars, the faster the wind).

CLOUDS

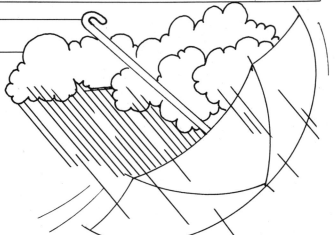

Cumulonimbus 1
Stratus. 2
Low, thickening. 3
High clouds 4
Stratocumulus 5
Clouds rising 5
Clear 6
Cumulus 7

WINDS

N 2
NE 1
E 1
SE 1
S 2
SW 3
W. 3
NW 4
Variable. 3
Calm 3

PRESSURE

Very low and dropping. 1
Low and dropping. 2
Low and fluctuating 3
Average and dropping 3
High and dropping 3
Very high and dropping 4
Average, fluctuating. 5
Low, rising 6
Average and rising. 7
High and rising 8
Very high and rising 9

WEATHER FORECASTER

Forecast #	Forecast
3	Heavy precipitation within six hours
4	Precipitation within 6-12 hours, little temperature change
5	Brief precipitation within 18 hours, rise in temperature
6 or 7	Precipitation within 24 hours, rise in temperature
8	Precipitation within 30 hours, no temperature change
9 or 10	Increase in clouds
11	Little precipitation in next 24 hours
12	Winds with possible showers
13 or 14	Immediate precipitation, then clearing and cooler
15	Showers or flurries, then clearing and cooler
16	Clearing in a few hours
17	Partly cloudy, no temperature change
18	Fair with little change in next 36 hours
19	Mostly fair with rising temperatures
20	Continued fair

PEOPLE AND WEATHER

It was a tough year for Orville Cranesboggle. His tomatoes didn't get enough rain. A cold snap ruined the orange crop in Florida, so the cost of orange juice jumped 27¢ a gallon. (And Orville loves orange juice.) He bought skis and it never snowed. A hailstorm in August smashed his cucumbers and zinnias. A tornado blew away his aunt's barn and her two hogs. It poured on his company picnic, and there was a flash flood on Halloween. What a year!

Just like Orville, we're all affected by the weather every day of our lives. It influences what we wear, where we live, what we buy, and where we go. Studies have shown that the weather may even affect our moods and our health. In fact, there's a branch of meteorology called *biometeorology* that studies how the weather affects living things.

Getting a Grip on the Weather: Witch doctors, medicine men, rain dancers, and magicians have long tried to change the weather. But now scientists have gotten into the "weather-changing" business. In the 1940s the first successful cloud seeding was performed when scientists found that shooting tiny crystals of silver iodide or dry ice into a supercooled cloud could make it rain or snow. Since then, scientists have tried to:
- improve cloud seeding techniques
- break up hailstorms
- reduce the strength of hurricanes
- get rid of thick fog

The benefits of changing the weather are obvious—making more rain could end droughts and increase crop production. And reducing the power of hurricanes and hailstorms could save lives and property. But changing the weather also brings up controversial social, environmental, and political issues. Creating good weather for one state might bring dangerous weather to another. For example, if someone seeds clouds to make it rain in Texas, but there are flash floods in Oklahoma, what's been gained? And how do you prove anyone's to blame? The flash floods *might* have happened with or without cloud seeding.

Weather changes can also affect other countries. If hurricanes headed for Texas are diverted, then Mexico's Gulf Coast, which needs the rain from these storms, might lose out. Scientists know that much more research is needed before we can make changes in the weather and understand the consequences. And even if we did understand exactly what effect the weather changes would have, there would still be social, environmental, and political issues to deal with.

Climate vs Weather: Climate and weather are two words that are often used interchangeably. But they are not the same. Weather is the state of the atmosphere at a particular time, and climate is the average weather in an area over a long period of time. For example, the climate in some parts of Hawaii is hot and humid with a lot of rainfall all year long. But the weather today on Waikiki Beach may be sunny and mild.

(continued on next page)

Changing Climates: Fifteen thousand years ago the northern part of North America was covered with huge sheets of ice, and the overall temperature of the earth was cooler than it is today. (There were still warm and humid climates on the earth, but the average temperature in many areas was cooler than it is today.) From the time the earth first formed, its climates have been changing slowly—sometimes getting warmer and sometimes getting cooler. And many are changing right now. Scientists still don't know exactly why there are large-scale climate changes on the earth. But they do know that the changes seem to occur in cycles that vary from a few years to millions of years in length.

Some scientists think the earth's climates change because the energy from the sun changes. Others think the amount of volcanic dust in the air changes and affects the earth's overall climate. And others think the slow changes in the earth's orbit cause gradual shifts in the earth's climate. But most scientists think there's just not enough evidence yet to prove any of these ideas.

Now some scientists are concerned that people may be affecting weather patterns. Air pollution and the deforestation of huge areas of the tropics could be changing the composition of the atmosphere, which could eventually affect the earth's overall climate.

A Rising Problem: Fuels are burning all over the world—in furnaces, wood stoves, outdoor grills, cars, trucks, planes, and incinerators. As fuels burn, carbon dioxide is added to the air, along with other gases and tiny particles.

Over time some of these by-products build up and interact with weather elements to create problems such as *acid rain* (rain mixed with sulfur dioxide and other chemicals that are very harmful to living things) and *smog* (fog, smoke, and noxious chemicals trapped at low levels in the atmosphere).

Meteorologists and other scientists are concerned with the long-range problems of air pollution as well as the short-term ones. Some worry that all the extra carbon dioxide being dumped into the atmosphere might trap heat and cause the earth to warm up. And most scientists are concerned about the depletion of the ozone layer in the earth's atmosphere, caused by the use of chemicals known as chlorofluorocarbons or CFCs. Since the ozone layer protects the earth from the sun's harmful ultraviolet (UV) rays, the consequences of ozone depletion could include an increase in UV-related problems, such as skin cancer and eye disease.

No one is sure exactly how our weather system will handle all these changes in the atmosphere or how these changes will affect our future. But it is a problem we need to learn more about and deal with now.

Weather on the Job

Discuss how weather affects different types of jobs.

Objective:
Describe how weather affects people at work.

Ages:
Primary

Materials:
- *grocery bags or construction paper*
- *scissors*
- *felt-tipped marker*
- *glue*
- *empty soft drink bottle*
- *crayons*
- *tape*
- *sheets of 8½ × 11" paper*

Subject:
Social Studies

What do farmers, painters, naturalists, pilots, firefighters, lifeguards, and letter carriers all have in common? They all keep an eye on the weather because their work depends on it.

Kids love to think about what they will be when they grow up. This activity will get them thinking about how the weather might affect their future jobs and how weather affects each of us every day.

Pick a Job!

naturalist	teacher
firefighter	musician
pilot	grocer
farmer	banker
lifeguard	gardener
letter carrier	sailor
angler	hockey player
writer	tennis player
doctor	baker
law officer	construction worker
judge	carpenter

Pass out crayons and a half sheet of paper to each person. Then divide the group into six teams. Have each member of each team draw something related to weather, such as sunshine, clouds, rain, snow, wind, fog, or lightning. For example, everybody in team one could draw windy day pictures, while those in team two could draw their versions of a rainy day.

While the teams are drawing pictures, you can make the game board using a large piece of construction paper or several grocery bags taped together. Cut out a large circle (with a diameter of about 50 inches [1.3 m]) and divide the circle into six segments using a ruler and a marking pen (see diagram). Then draw a smaller circle with an 8-inch (20-cm) diameter in the middle of the game board.

Tell the kids in team one to paste their drawings into one of the segments. Team two can paste their pictures into the next segment and so on until the game board is filled. Then set the bottle in the small circle so that it's in the center of the game board.

Next copy the various occupations listed to the left on slips of paper and add any others you can think of. Place the slips in a hat.

Have each of the kids pick a job out of the hat, one at a time, and read it to the rest of the group. (If the kids are too young to read or don't understand the job, you can read and discuss it with the group before going on.) Next have each person spin the bottle to see what kind of weather he or she will have on the job today. When the bottle stops ask each child these questions:
- What is the weather like for you today?
- What special clothes will you wear today?
- Will it be a nice day to be a ___?
- Will the weather help you do your job or will it make it harder?
- What's your favorite kind of weather?

You can make up other questions that will get them thinking about how the weather affects everyone.

Weather Scavenger Hunt

Search for weather-related clues outside.

Objective:
Describe several ways weather affects plants, soil, and people and other animals.

Ages:
All

Materials:
- *scavenger clue sheets*
- *bags*
- *pencils and paper*
- *clipboards*
- *rubber bands, tape, or glue (optional)*
- *sturdy cardboard*

Subject:
Science

Take your group on a weather scavenger hunt to see how many weather-related things they can find. Use the list of clues provided to make up a clue sheet that is appropriate for your group. Some of the clues don't require any weather background, but others do.

Divide your group into teams and give each team a clue sheet, a bag, a pencil, one or two sheets of paper, and a clipboard. (If you don't have clipboards, tape or glue the clue sheets to pieces of sturdy cardboard or attach with rubber bands.) Explain to the kids that they can put some of their "weather finds" in their bags. But for the clues they can't collect, they should draw or describe what they see on their blank sheets. (Young children can go on a weather scavenger hunt too—just take them for a walk and talk about some of the easier weather clues.)

Set a time for all the teams to meet back at the starting point. Then have each team show and explain what they found for each clue. Afterward, have each team return any "finds" to where the items were found.

Note: Before sending the group out, make sure to set your own scavenger hunt guidelines, such as: "Do not pick flowers, reach under logs with bare hands, or wander away from the rest of the group."

Clues

1. Something bending toward the sun
2. Something hiding from sunshine
3. Something that may become part of a cloud
4. Something that tells you the wind is blowing
5. Something left by the rain
6. A sign of an animal used in folklore to "predict" the weather
7. A bad place for a person to seek shelter during a lightning storm
8. A place where icicles might form
9. A place where weather has damaged a building
10. A good place for a person to seek shelter during a tornado
11. Sign of an animal that likes rain
12. A place to go where it's cool
13. A place where rain has moved the soil
14. A place that gets little sunshine
15. Something that bends in the wind
16. Something that won't bend in the wind
17. Something that reflects lots of sunlight
18. Something that absorbs lots of sunlight
19. Something that will soak up rain
20. Something that makes rain splatter
21. Something that protects people from rain
22. Something that uses sunlight or wind or water to work
23. Something that smells better after a rain shower
24. A good windbreak
25. Something shaped by wind or water
26. A sign of lightning damage
27. Something the color of the sky
28. Something the color of snow
29. Something that would make snow melt

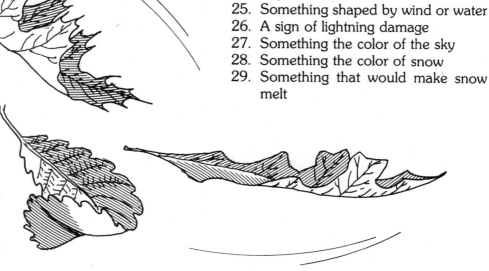

What Do You Think?

Take a poll to find out how people feel about the weather.

Objectives:
Discuss how people feel about different aspects of the weather. Define *majority* and *minority.*

Ages:
Intermediate and Advanced

Materials:
- paper
- pencils and pens

Subjects:
Language Arts, Math, and Science

How many people have seen a tornado? Or have been frightened by lightning? What kind of weather do most people like best? Do most people talk about the weather every day?

Your group can find out the answers to questions like these by making up a weather questionnaire and polling friends, families, and neighbors.

Divide your group into teams of two or three people. Tell them they will be making up a 10-question survey. They can include whatever weather-related questions they want, but remind them to:
- make the questions fairly short and easy to answer (Try to make them all yes/no questions or multiple choice questions.)
- record the age and sex of each person polled
- try to survey a mix of people (different ages, sexes, and so on)

You can also assign each group a general topic, such as pollution, weather preferences, storm safety, weather trivia, or climate, to explore with their questionnaires. Here are some sample questions:

1. Have you ever been in a tornado? (Repeat for hurricane, blizzard, and flash flood.)
2. Do you think acid rain is a serious problem in our environment?
3. If caught outdoors during a thunderstorm, which of the following is the safest place to stay?
   a. on a hill
   b. under a tall tree
   c. in a low-lying area
4. Do you know someone who can predict a change in the weather by "feeling" it in his or her bones?
5. When did you first notice the weather today?
   a. when you woke up
   b. when you decided what to wear
   c. when you walked outside
6. Do you think scientists should try to change the paths of hurricanes or seed clouds to make it rain?
7. Can you name three songs about the weather?
8. Have you talked about the weather today?
9. What is a scientist who studies the atmosphere called?
10. Do you like rain?
11. Do you like snow?
12. What is your favorite type of weather?

After all the teams have finished writing their questionnaires, have them go out and start interviewing. (Make sure each team polls the same number of people so you can compare results.) After the polling is done, have each team tally up their results and report back to the rest of the group.

BRANCHING OUT: MATH

To make the polls official, have your kids calculate some survey statistics. They can figure out:
- what percentage of people polled answered *yes* to each question as opposed to *no* (or *a, b,* or *c* for multiple choice questions)
- what percentage of males answered *yes* or *no* to each question as opposed to females
- what percentage of the people polled were males and what percentage were females
- the average age of the people polled

Here's an example:

Out of 10 people polled, four answered *yes* to the question, "Have you talked about the weather today?" To figure out the percentage of the people who said *yes,* divide 4 by 10 and then multiply by 100. That will give you 40%.

Six people, or 60%, hadn't talked about the weather before the poll. So more people answered *no* to the question than answered *yes,* showing that the *majority* of people polled had not discussed the weather. The people who had talked about the weather were in the *minority.*

The Weather Zapper: A Radio Play to Finish

Write an ending to a weather radio play and then perform the play.

Objectives:

Develop an ending to a radio play about weather control. Discuss some of the pros and cons of controlling the weather.

Ages:

Intermediate and Advanced

Materials:

- *ruler or yardstick*
- *box filled with jars, dishes, stones, and cans*
- *blender or hot air popcorn popper*
- *shoes*
- *radio*
- *tape recorder*
- *microphone*
- *copies of the play on pages 55–57*

Subjects:

Drama, Creative Writing, and Science

What would happen to the world if someone could "control" or modify our weather? Could long-term weather modification affect our climate? Could it help us wipe out droughts and prevent deaths from raging storms?

These are some of the questions that scientists have been thinking about since the first cloud seeding experiments began in the 1940s. Since then, many weather modification experiments have been conducted. But none of the experiments have been as successful as many scientists hoped they would be.

As water shortages continue to be a growing problem some scientists think there will be an increased interest in weather modification experiments and a need for them to continue. They feel we need to keep experimenting so we can learn more about how the weather works and how we can influence it to help save lives and bring rain to areas that need water.

Other scientists feel weather control won't ever work—we just won't ever know enough about how the atmosphere works to successfully control it. And if we *could* control it, we might create more problems than we solve.

Discuss some of the controversy surrounding weather control with your group. You might also want to discuss these related topics:

- **Air Pollution:** Discuss how people have already affected the weather by polluting the air. As we add more substances to the atmosphere, we change the chemical balance in the air, and this could create changes in our weather patterns. Acid rain and chemical smog are two examples of serious air pollution problems.

- **Is the Earth Getting Colder or Warmer?:** Discuss how air pollution and other factors might be changing our climate. For example, some people say another Ice Age is coming because air pollution in the atmosphere is blocking out some of the sun's energy. Others say just the opposite. They think all the carbon dioxide and other gases being dumped into the air from exhausts and smokestacks may be keeping the earth's heat from escaping into space, thus raising the earth's overall temperature. (This is called the *greenhouse effect* because the carbon dioxide is thought to act like the walls and ceiling of a greenhouse in trapping warm air.)

After discussing weather modification, try putting on the "Weather Zapper" radio play (on pages 55–57) with your group. But first hold a "finish the radio play" contest. (You can have the kids work individually or in teams.) Have each team or person read the play (or read it to them yourself) and then have each of them write an exciting ending to the story. If the kids are working in teams, each team can put on their own production of the play using their own special ending. Afterward, you can take a vote to see which ending is the "winner." If the kids are working individually, pick one or two winning endings and use these endings when you put on the play.

PUTTING ON THE PLAY

Radio plays can be a lot of fun. You don't have to worry about costumes, make-up, or even memorizing your lines. But radio plays are a challenge. Since no one can see the characters, the radio actors must project the personalities of their characters through their voices.

Radio plays also use sound effects to help dramatize the action. Footsteps, thunder, rain, wind, motors, fighting, and other sounds can be imitated by a well-equipped sound effects team.

In this play we have ten characters listed. (More might be written in by the authors of the endings.) You will also need someone to work the tape recorder or microphones, another (the director) to follow along with the script and cue in the actors and sound effects team, and several people to handle the sound effects table. (If necessary, one person can play more than one part by disguising his or her voice.)

After the plays are taped, let the teams lean back, munch on some popcorn, and listen to their productions.

THE WEATHER ZAPPER: A RADIO PLAY

Characters:
- *Dr. El Niño*
- *Buster Bora*
- *Gerry Greedstone*
- *Gale*
- *Glazer*
- *News Reporter*
- *Ed Front*
- *Elizabeth Hale Hodgson*
- *Narrator I*
- *Narrator II*

Stagehands:
- *Stage Director*
- *Sound Effects Team*

(All sound effects and stage cues are in parentheses.)

Bruce Norfleet

(Soft music can be playing in the background as the narrator introduces the play.)

Narrator I: Good evening, ladies and gentlemen, and welcome to tonight's radio play, "The Weather Zapper." It is a story about a brilliant scientist who discovers an amazing way to control the weather. We hope you'll enjoy tonight's exciting adventure.

Scene I: Dr. El Niño's Laboratory

Narrator II: Dr. El Niño, a world renowned weather scientist, is working late one night in his research lab in southern Kentucky. His assistant, Buster Bora, is helping him with a new invention.

Dr. El Niño: Come here quickly, Buster. (heavy footsteps) I think I've finally perfected the Weather Zapper!

Buster: What great news, Dr. El Niño! How will it work?

Dr. El Niño: It's pretty complicated, Buster. But if I shoot this special chemical—tetraethyl dibromyl sulfurine bimethyl—into the sky, I can make it rain just by adjusting the controls. And I can also create huge swirling winds that can push tornadoes and hurricanes off their courses to save towns from disaster.

Buster: Wow! What an invention! But how can you control it?

Dr. El Niño: All I have to do is set these four controls and shoot the chemical into the right type of cloud. Then whammo!

Buster: Just think, Doctor—flash floods, tornadoes, hurricanes, and droughts can all be disasters of the past. (A door slams.)

Dr. El Niño: Who would be here at this hour? (Heavy footsteps pound up the stairs.)

Dr. El Niño: Quick, Buster, hide the Weather Zapper in that drawer and lock it. No one must know we have it until it is tested. (A drawer slams, the door opens, and three people storm in. Footsteps.)

Gerry Greedstone: Too late, my clever Doctor. I know you have the Zapper. We've bugged your lab for the last three months. Now where is it?

Dr. El Niño: Who are you, and what gives you the right to barge in here like this? *(continued on next page)*

Gerry: My name is Gerry Greedstone, and these are my two assistants Gale and Glazer. When I heard that you were researching a weather controller, I knew I had to get my hands on it. With this Weather Zapper I will be rich. (laughs an evil laugh) Now I will be the only person in the universe who can control the weather, and people will do whatever I say!

Dr. El Niño: You're a fool, Greedstone. The Weather Zapper hasn't even been tested. Besides, you don't know how to use it. I warn you, it can turn on you.

Gerry: It's too late, Doc. Gale, Glazer, quick—tie them up and find the Weather Zapper. (First, the sounds of shuffling and fighting: Shake a big box filled with cans, stones, jars, and other junk. Then the sound of a gunshot: Slap a yardstick or ruler on a table.)

Buster: Oh, no—they've shot the lock off the drawer. And they've got the Zapper!

Gerry: Come on, you guys. Let's get out of here before we get caught. (footsteps running downstairs)

(Imitate a motor by running a blender or a hot air popcorn popper, or by saying "varoommmmm.") Hurry! Try to loosen your ropes, Buster. We need to get to the police! (grunts and gasps, heavy breathing)

Buster: I've done it, sir. I've slipped the ropes off. Here, I'll untie you, and we'll call the police. Don't worry, sir!

Scene II: Radio Station Newsroom

Narrator I: News of the Weather Zapper has spread quickly—no one knows where or when the first "zap" will take place. Dr. El Niño and Buster, along with meteorologists all over the world, keep watching the sky and listening to the news. In a few days strange reports start pouring in. (music playing)

Reporter: We interrupt this program to bring you a special news flash from Hawaii. We now switch to our Hawaii correspondent, Ed Front.

Bruce Norfleet

Dr. El Niño: We're in deep, deep trouble, Buster. With that Zapper they can change the world's weather in a flash. And I don't think they will use it to help people.

Buster: There's always a chance it won't work, isn't there?

Dr. El Niño: Yes, I suppose there's always a chance. There they go, Buster.

Ed: Hawaii's never seen anything like this, folks. It's been snowing in Honolulu for over three hours. The palm trees and beaches are covered with snow. There are already three inches on the ground and chilling winds are blowing! (blow on the mike) Brrrrr! And the weather's getting worse by the minute.

Reporter: Thank you, Ed. And now we take you to our London correspondent, Elizabeth Hale Hodgson.

Elizabeth: I say, this is the strangest thing. A tornado has just touched down near Buckingham Palace. The queen and her family have managed to escape the storm with no harm. Oh, no—I see another funnel cloud . . . *hellllllp!* (loud wind—blow on mike)

Reporter: The world's weather seems to be in an uproar. Skies are being zapped everywhere. Who's doing this and what's the reason? We'll have more on the eleven o'clock news tonight. Now back to our program. (more music and then fade out)

Scene III: Back in the Lab

Narrator II: Meanwhile, back in the lab, Dr. El Niño and Buster work through the night, trying to figure out a solution to the world's weather mess.

Dr. El Niño: I've got a plan, Buster. I know how to stop them before they do more damage and kill innocent people.

Buster: How, Doctor?

Now you finish the play!

Weagevia

eagevia (wee-JEE-vee-uh) is a lively game that combines interesting **wea**ther tri**via** with worldwide **ge**ography.

Cut out the bits of weather trivia listed on page 58 and put them into a hat. Divide your group into five teams and give each team a number from one to five. They will keep these numbers throughout the game. (You can also play the game with two teams.)

To start, have one member from the first team draw a slip of weather trivia and read it to the entire group. Each bit of trivia will include the name of a country, a state, or a province. After the team hears the question, they have one minute to decide where the place is located on the world or U.S. map. The team member who drew the trivia then has 30 seconds to pin (or tape) the trivia to the right spot on the map. If he or she pins it to the right place, the team gets five points for a state or province and 10 points for a foreign country.

If the first team misses, team two then gets a chance at the same weather trivia, but for one less point (four points for a state or province and nine points for a foreign country). Continue until the weather trivia is worth zero points or until you get back to team one. Then start a new round with the next team. (Be sure each person has a chance to pick, read, and pin up at least one bit of weather trivia.)

TRIVIA TIPS

- Try to use maps that do not have the countries, states, or provinces labeled.
- You will probably need a U.S. map in addition to a world map because the states are usually too small to locate on a world map. (The Canadian provinces are usually large enough to identify on a world map.)
- Have the kids add their own weather trivia to the game.

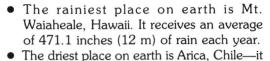

- The rainiest place on earth is Mt. Waiaheale, Hawaii. It receives an average of 471.1 inches (12 m) of rain each year.
- The driest place on earth is Arica, Chile—it gets an average of only .03 inch (.8 mm) of rain a year.
- The *southeaster* is a strong wind that blows over the Cape of Good Hope, South Africa.
- In Scotland a gentle breeze is known as a *waff*.
- Silver Lake, Colorado, holds the record for the most snow during a 24-hour period. An incredible 75.8 inches (1.9 m) of snow blanketed this small mountain city on April 14, 1921.
- The *surazo* is an icy cold wind that blows over the Andes Plateau in Peru.
- The largest-recorded hailstone fell at Coffeyville, Kansas, on March 9, 1970. It weighed 1.7 pounds (0.8 kg), measured 7.5 inches (19 cm) in diameter, and had a circumference of 17.5 inches (44 cm).
- On June 19, 1932, a hailstorm in the Hunan Province of China killed 200 people and injured thousands more.
- The hottest place in the world is Dallol, Ethiopia. Between the years 1960 and 1966, the average daily maximum temperature was 100° F (38° C) every month of the year except December, when it was 98° F (37° C), and January, when it was 97° F (36° C).
- The highest temperature recorded for one day was 136° F (58° C) in Azizia, Libya, on September 13, 1922.
- The highest temperature reached for one day in North America was 134° F (57° C) in Death Valley, California, on July 10, 1913.
- The highest temperature recorded in Antarctica was 58° F (14° C) at Esperanza, on the Antarctic Peninsula.
- A *bad-i-sad-o-bistroz* is a violent wind that blows from the mountains of Afghanistan.
- Thunder is heard an average of 242 days each year in Kamala, Uganda.
- The people of Saudi Arabia call the strong northern winds that often carry lots of sand *belots* (BEE-lows).
- The first weather maps published were sold to the public for one penny at the Great Exhibition of 1851 in London, England.
- When a city the size of Chicago, Illinois, gets 1 inch (2.5 cm) of rain, over four billion gallons (15 billion l) of water fall.

- The Empire State Building of New York City has been hit by lightning 42 times in one year, 12 times in one storm, and nine times in a 20-minute period.
- Monsoon winds bring heavy rains to India during the summer months. An average of 71 inches (178 cm) of rain falls each year in Bombay, India, and 98% of the rain falls during the monsoon season.
- William A. Bentley of Vermont was the first person to photograph snow crystals with a camera fixed to a microscope. Bentley built up a collection of over 6000 photographs of snow crystals.
- The dry winds that blow dust and sand across desert areas in Egypt are called *haboobs*.
- The very strong and sudden winds that bring thunderstorms to northwestern Australia are known as *Cockeyed Bobs*.
- The winds that bring cold, polar air to northern Japan are called *narais* (nar-AZ).
- The violent winds that sweep across the pampas of Argentina are called *pamperos*.
- The "Pole of Cold" in Vostok, Antarctica, is considered the coldest place in the world. The average temperature for a year there is -72° F (-58° C) and temperatures in July average -130° F (-90° C). (July is a winter month in the Southern Hemisphere.)
- In Verhoyansh, Siberia, temperatures range from -90° F (-68° C) in the winter to 98° F (37° C) in the summer.
- The greatest range in temperature for one day was recorded in Browning, Montana. On January 23 the temperature was 44° F (7° C) and within 24 hours the temperature dropped to -56° F (-49° C).
- The Montgolfier brothers of France invented a hot air balloon that was the forerunner of the weather balloons we use today. Their balloon was first launched in 1783.

CRAFTY CORNER

Here are some weather art and craft ideas you can use to complement many of the activities in the first five chapters.

Fogged-Up Pictures

Make foggy scenes with wax paper.

Ages:
Primary and Intermediate

Materials:
- **wax paper**
- **brown, gray, and black construction paper**
- **glue**
- **scissors**
- **stapler**

Subjects:
Art and Crafts

Here's how to make a great-looking fog scene:
1. Cut trees, mountains, and other scenery from construction paper.
2. Glue the scenery to another piece of construction paper. (Gray works best for a foggy scene.) *Note:* Leave a half-inch (1.3-cm) border on the two short sides of the picture.
3. Cut a piece of wax paper the size of the construction paper. Lay the wax paper over the scenery and glue it to the construction paper by putting a dab of glue on each corner.

4. Cut trees, grass, and other foreground scenery from construction paper. Glue the scenery on top of the wax paper.
5. Cut two black construction paper borders, each about 1½ inches (4 cm) wide. Each border should be as long as one of the short sides of the picture.
6. Fold each of the borders in half over the short sides of the picture and staple them to the picture in two or three places. Your foggy scene is now complete!

Idea reprinted with permission from *The Little Kid's Four Seasons Craft Book,* Jackie Vermeer and Marian Lariviere (Taplinger Publishing Co., Inc. 1974).

Soda Straw Snowflakes

Cut up soda straws and glue the pieces down in snowflake patterns.

Ages:
Intermediate and Advanced

Materials:
- **aluminum foil**
- **plastic straws (white, clear, or colored)**
- **ballpoint pens (enough for everyone)**
- **scissors**
- **Tacky glue or some other thick white glue**
- **string or yarn**

Subject:
Crafts

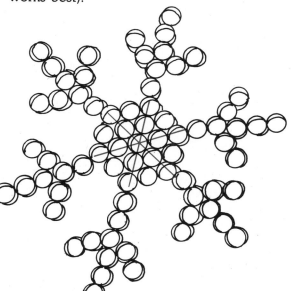

Here's a different way for children to make snowflakes. Give each child eight to 10 plastic straws and a piece of foil about 8 inches (20 cm) square. Also make sure everyone has a ballpoint pen, a pair of scissors, and some glue (thick white glue works best).

Here's how to do it:
1. Cut the straws into pieces about ¼ inch (6 mm) long. (You may want to mark them with a ballpoint pen beforehand to make sure the pieces are the same size.)
2. Mark three evenly-spaced, intersecting lines on the foil (see diagram). The lines should be about 5 inches (13 cm) long, intersecting at the 2½-inch (6.5-cm) mark. The points of the lines mark the six points of the snowflake.
3. Starting at the center, go over one of the six lines with a thick line of glue. Then place the straw pieces along the line. As you go, put a thin line of glue along each side of each straw piece so that each piece will stick to its neighbor. (This will make the snowflake stronger.) Finish gluing along all of the lines and let the snowflakes dry completely. (Overnight should do it.)

(continued on next page)

4. When the snowflakes are dry, cut the excess foil from around the six points and attach a piece of string or yarn through one of the top straw pieces. (If you use Tacky glue or another special kind of thick white glue, you can remove the whole snowflake from the foil. Just *carefully* slide a table knife between the snowflake and the foil. But this works only with special, super-stick white glues. Glues that don't stick as well will allow the snowflakes to fall apart if you try to remove the foil backing.)

Soda straw snowflakes make great tree ornaments. Or you can hang several of them at different lengths in front of a window. Encourage the children to make a lot of different snowflake designs—just remind them that each flake should have six sides.

Taken with permission from *Young Naturalist* by Ilo Hiller, published by Texas A&M University Press, 1983.

Make a Wind Sock

Make a wind sock to record wind direction and wind speed.

Ages:
Intermediate and Advanced

Materials:
- *cotton cloth (1 square yard [0.8 m²] will make a large wind sock.)*
- *sturdy wire (A piece 18 inches [45 cm] long will fit a large wind sock.)*
- *nylon fishing line (10 feet [3 m])*
- *wooden post or garden stake (about 7 feet [2 m] long)*
- *hammer*
- *nail (2 to 3 inches [5 to 8 cm] long)*
- *needle and thread*
- *thumbtacks*
- *scissors*
- *waterproof markers*

Subject:
Crafts

Here's how to make a wind sock to measure wind direction and wind speed:
1. Cut the cloth into a triangle and sew two sides together so that the cloth is cone-shaped.
2. Bend the wire into a circle and wrap the two ends around each other.
3. Fold the open end of the cloth over the wire and sew the cloth as shown in the diagram. (You may need to adjust the size of the wire circle before you sew to make sure the cloth fits over it well.)

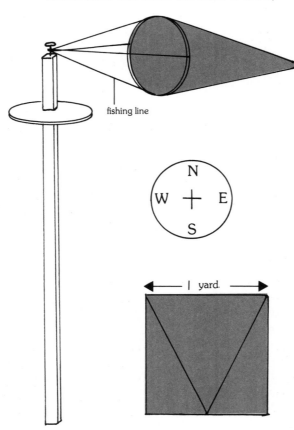

fishing line

4. Poke four equally spaced holes in the cloth, each about 1½ inches (4 cm) from the edge. Tie a 2-foot (60-cm) length of fishing line to each hole (see diagram).
5. Cut out a cardboard circle, 12 inches (30 cm) in diameter. Make an X in the center of the circle by cutting two 1-inch (2.5-cm) slits.
6. At the outer edge and on both sides of the circle, write the letters N, S, E, and W (see diagram). Make the letters big and colorful.
7. Slide the cardboard circle down about a foot (30 cm) or so onto the post or stake. Then thumbtack the slit edges of the circle to the post.
8. Work out a wind speed scale for your wind sock by holding it out the window of a moving car on a calm day and noting its angle at different speeds. On a sheet of paper, draw diagrams of the wind sock's angle at the different speeds, then refer to the sheet when you use your wind sock.
9. Drive the nail into the end of the wooden post and push the post into the ground in an open area, making sure that the letters on the cardboard circle point in the right directions. Then tie the four loose ends of the fishing line onto the nail.

Remember, wind direction is specified according to the direction the wind is coming *from*. When the wind blows, the *open* end of the sock will face that direction.

APPENDIX

Questions, Questions, and More Questions

1. Water can be a solid, a liquid, or a ____. (vapor)
2. Water from rivers, lakes, plants, and animals ____ and rises into the atmosphere. (evaporates)
3. Rain, drizzle, snow, sleet, and hail are all forms of ____. (precipitation)
4. A cloud at ground level is called ____. (fog)
5. The ocean of air that surrounds the earth is called the ____. (atmosphere)
6. The barometer reading usually ____ before a storm. (falls)
7. The energy from the ____ causes the wind to blow. (sun)
8. A scientist who studies the atmosphere is called a ____. (meteorologist)
9. Cold air weighs ____ than warm air. (more)
10. In the United States, weather usually moves from ____ to ____. (west, east)
11. ____ pressure systems usually bring wet or stormy weather. (Low)
12. Name the four things that together cause our weather. (the sun, the earth, air, and water)
13. When it's winter in Canada, is the Northern Hemisphere tilted toward or away from the sun? (away)
14. Which is there more of in the atmosphere: oxygen, nitrogen, or carbon dioxide? (nitrogen)
15. Name five layers of the atmosphere. (Troposphere, stratosphere, ionosphere, mesosphere, thermosphere, and exosphere are some of the layers meteorologists have designated.)
16. Do hurricanes form over land or over water? (water)
17. Which can hold more water vapor—warm or cold air? (warm)
18. Name two local or regional winds and where they occur. (See page 58 for examples.)
19. In which layer of the atmosphere does most of our weather occur? (troposphere)
20. As you climb a mountain, does the air pressure increase or decrease? (decrease)
21. Name three of the weather instruments usually found at a weather station. (hygrometer, barometer, thermometer, psychrometer, anemometer, and so on)
22. If you get caught in a thunderstorm, a safe place to wait out the storm is under a tree. (False. Lightning typically strikes tall objects such as trees.)
23. In a thunderstorm, you usually hear thunder rumble before you see lightning flash. (False. Light travels faster than sound, so lightning can be seen before thunder can be heard.)
24. Thunder is a noise made by clouds bumping into each other. (False. The noise we call thunder occurs when air expands and vibrates during a lightning flash.)
25. Dewdrops are very tiny raindrops that fall from the sky just before dawn. (False. Dew doesn't fall at all. It forms when water vapor in the air condenses on grass and other objects on or near the ground.)
26. A warm front occurs when a warm air mass moves under a cold air mass. (False. A warm front occurs when a warm air mass replaces a cold air mass.)
27. Plowed fields absorb more of the sun's heat than sandy deserts do. (True, because plowed fields are usually darker.)
28. Cloudy nights are usually warmer than clear nights. (True. Clouds keep some of the earth's heat from escaping into space.)
29. Land heats up and cools down faster than water. (True.)
30. The climate of North America has been the same for millions of years. (False. North America's climate has become warmer and cooler many times. During the Ice Ages, many areas of North America were covered with ice.)
31. Acid rain occurs when rain containing acidic chemicals falls to the earth. (True.)

Glossary

air mass—a large body of air that has nearly the same temperature and humidity at the same altitude throughout.

atmosphere—the "ocean" of gases that surrounds the earth. The atmosphere is often classified into five layers: the troposphere, the stratosphere, the mesosphere, the thermosphere, and the exosphere.

coalescence—the growth of a tiny cloud droplet, by collision with other droplets, into a raindrop heavy enough to fall from a cloud.

condense—to change from a vapor to a liquid.

dew point—the temperature at which air can't hold any more moisture (i.e., relative humidity is 100%) and the water vapor in it condenses. When air reaches its dew point, clouds, fog, or dew can form.

doldrums—a nearly windless region that extends approximately 700 miles (1120 km) north and south of the equator.

evaporate—to change from a liquid to a vapor.

exosphere—the outermost layer of the atmosphere.

fog—a cloud in contact with the ground.

front—the boundary between air masses of different temperatures and humidities. A cold front forms when a cold air mass pushes into a warm air mass, and a warm front forms when a warm air mass replaces a retreating cold air mass.

greenhouse effect—the warming of the earth that occurs when the atmosphere traps heat waves radiated from the earth in much the same way that heat in a greenhouse is trapped by the glass walls and roof.

high pressure system— an area of above-normal pressure. In the Northern Hemisphere, winds of a high pressure system spiral clockwise and outward; in the Southern Hemisphere they spiral counterclockwise and outward. A high pressure system usually brings fair weather. Also known as a *High* or *anti-cyclone*.

humidity—the amount of water vapor in the air. The *relative humidity* is the amount of water vapor in the air compared to the maximum the air could hold at that temperature, expressed as a percentage.

ionosphere—the layer of the atmosphere named for the electrically charged atoms or molecules (ions) it contains. The ionosphere can overlap some other atmospheric layers.

jet stream—a ribbon of high-speed winds that blows high above the earth in the upper troposphere.

low pressure system— an area of below-normal pressure. In the Northern Hemisphere, winds of a low pressure system spiral counterclockwise and inward; in the Southern Hemisphere they spiral clockwise and inward. A low pressure system usually brings stormy weather. Also known as a *Low* or *cyclone*.

mesosphere—the layer of the atmosphere that lies above the stratosphere.

meteorology—the study of the state of the atmosphere and of weather forecasting. A scientist who studies meteorology is called a *meteorologist*.

prevailing winds—winds that blow more or less steadily from a specific direction. The three main prevailing winds are the *trade winds,* the *polar easterlies,* and the *prevailing westerlies.*

stratosphere—the layer of the atmosphere that lies above the troposphere.

supercooled—the condition in which water remains in a liquid form at below-freezing temperatures.

thermosphere—the layer of the atmosphere that lies above the mesosphere.

troposphere—the layer of the atmosphere that lies closest to the earth. Most of our weather occurs in the troposphere.

1997 UPDATE

TABLE OF CONTENTS

TORNADOES!

Every spring, the middle part of the United States gets ready for Mother Nature's most destructive force on earth—the tornado! Tornadoes are really fast spinning funnels of air that cause great damage on the ground. Tornadoes have been known to take roofs off of houses, throw cars through the air, and toss trains off their tracks. Tornadoes have done even stranger things, too, like plucking the feathers out of chickens and driving pieces of grass into tree trunks. There even might have been a tornado or two that picked up a cow and sent it sailing through the air!

Many years ago, lots of people died or were hurt by tornadoes. These days, a lot fewer people are killed by tornadoes. Why? Because scientists have learned a lot about them and can alert people before they are hit by the twisters. That gives people a lot more time to take shelter from the storms. But how have scientists learned more about tornadoes?

Chasing Storms

About 25 years ago, a place called the National Severe Storms Laboratory in Norman, Oklahoma, thought of a really cool idea to study tornadoes. They decided it would be neat if scientists could drive right out to the tornadoes, take pictures of them, and see them in person! This is what became known as "storm chasing," much like what the scientists did in the movie "Twister."

At the same time that scientists were chasing the tornadoes across the Great Plains, other scientists back at the laboratory were using a new machine called a Doppler radar to watch the storms that were making the tornadoes. The Doppler radar is a big spinning dish inside a round building that can detect severe storms many miles away. The Doppler radar can even "see" inside the thunderstorm and detect the rotation that happens just before the tornado touches down.

Through many years of chasing and watching the storms on the Doppler radar, scientists were able to write computer programs that could automatically detect the tornadoes, so that the public could be warned to take shelter.

Scientists used other devices to learn about tornadoes, too. They developed a big heavy machine that could be driven in front of the tornado to measure the winds, temperature, and air pressure inside the tornado. They called this machine "TOTO," and it looked very similar to "Dorothy" in the movie "Twister."

A few years ago, a huge storm chasing project called VORTEX was done in Texas, Kansas, and Oklahoma. VORTEX gathered tons of readings from more than 20 cars and vans, and scientists are using the data to learn even more about tornadoes. VORTEX scientists even built a Doppler radar on wheels that they could drive to almost 2 miles from the tornadoes! We have learned that tornadoes have "eyes" just like hurricanes, although tornadoes are a lot smaller.

Tornadoes and You

So, what can you do to save your family and friends from being hurt or killed by tornadoes? First, you should remember that most tornadoes happen in the spring months (March, April, May, and June), most tornadoes happen in the afternoon (from about 2 o'clock to about 6 o'clock), and most tornadoes happen in the middle states of America (Texas, Oklahoma, Kansas, Nebraska, Iowa). But, this does not mean tornadoes happen only at those times and at those places. They have been known to touch down in all 50 states, at all times of the year, and at any time of day. You should always be prepared for a tornado, no matter where you live.

How do you know a tornado is about to hit? Your town may have tornado sirens that will go off if a tornado is sighted nearby or detected on Doppler radar. Television and radio stations will sometimes tell you that a tornado has been sighted near your town. Some television stations in the middle part of the country will show tornadoes as they are happening! It all sounds really cool, but if there is a tornado warning for your town, you should stop watching the TV and take cover.

Where do you go? Well, if you are caught outside, you should try to get inside. If you can, do it in less than a minute. If not, then take shelter in a ditch. Never stay in your car. Most people who die during tornadoes are in their cars. That's because tornadoes pick up cars and toss them like matchboxes, crushing them instantly.

If you are inside, you should go to the basement and get under a stairwell or a heavy workbench, table, or desk. If you don't have a basement, then you should get into the center of your house, away from windows and doors leading outside. Your best spot is in a closet or bathroom. Always cover your face with your hands or with a towel. Most injuries are caused by small pieces of wood or glass being blown by winds over 100 miles per hour.

What can you do to learn more about tornadoes? One thing you could do is watch television or a weather channel, see where and when tornadoes have occurred, and mark them on a calendar. You can then see that most tornadoes occur in the spring, but that some occur at other times of the year. Another fun thing to do is to video record tornadoes from the television and create a collection of tornado videos. You could also create tornadoes by pulling the drain plug out of a bathtub or sink filled with water, and watching the water spin as it goes down the drain. However, kids should never chase tornadoes. It is too dangerous and should be done only by adults who know a lot about how tornadoes move and behave. If you don't know how a tornado acts, you could become one of its victims.

Remember, tornadoes are nature's most dangerous storms. They should be treated with respect. In the meantime, scientists are always learning more about them. Soon, we hope that there will be a day when tornadoes stop killing people.

Objective:

Make a barometer to measure fluctuations in air pressure and to tell when a low-pressure or high-pressure front has passed through your area.

Materials:

- large glass jar
- large, uninflated balloon
- rubber band
- masking tape
- toothpick
- 3-inch-by-5-inch card
- white glue
- pencil

PROCEDURE

1. See Figure 1-1.
2. Be sure the jar is clean and dry.
3. Cut off the neck of the balloon. Discard the neck.
4. Evenly stretch the remainder of the balloon over the jar.
5. Secure with a rubber band.
6. Glue the toothpick onto the balloon.
7. With tape, mount the card on the side of the jar.
8. Above the toothpick, write the word "High."
9. Below the toothpick, write the word "Low."
10. Place the barometer indoors away from moisture, heat, or windows. Be sure to keep it at a constant temperature.
11. Observe the barometer daily for any changes. See Figures 1-2 and 1-3 for examples.

High pressure exists when the outside air pressure is greater than the pressure inside the glass jar.

Low pressure exists when the outside air pressure is less than the pressure inside the glass jar.

3-inch-by-5-inch card — High

Drop of glue

Rubber band — Low

Balloon —

Jar —

Toothpick

1-1 Construction model

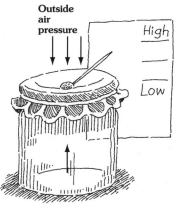

Outside air pressure

High

Low

1-2 Barometer high reading

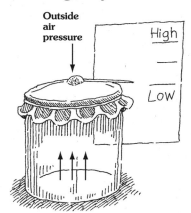

Outside air pressure

High

Low

1-3 Barometer low reading

GOING FURTHER

How will heat and cold affect the reading of this barometer? Place it in a refrigerator. Wait approximately 30 minutes. Remove the barometer and place it in a pan of hot water (approximately 35° Celsius, 95° Fahrenheit). How quickly did the pressure change?

QUESTION

1. When your barometer pointed to Low, what was the weather like within one to two days?

Raindrops reach a maximum size before breaking into smaller drops. Contrary to popular belief, falling rain is not teardrop shaped. See Figure 1-1 for examples. In this activity, you'll calculate raindrop size.

SHAPES OF FALLING RAINDROPS (NOT ACTUAL SIZE IN THESE DRAWINGS)

At diameters of .08 inches or less, a falling drop looks like this:

◯ (larger sphere)

Larger than this, but less than a ¼-inch in diameter, the drop bulges:

The air pressure flattens the bottom.

At diameters greater than ¼ inch, the droplet breaks up:

◯ ◯ (two or more smaller spheres)

1-1 Shapes of falling drops

Objective:
"Capture" several raindrops and calculate their volumes.

Materials:
- old nylon hose
- rubber band
- wide-mouthed glass jar
- flour
- centimeter ruler
- pencil
- calculator
- rainy day

PROCEDURE

1. See Figure 1-2.
2. Cut a 15-centimeter-by-15-centimeter square into the nylon hose.
3. Stretch the nylon tightly over the jar's mouth.
4. With a rubber band, securely attach the nylon to the glass jar.
5. Dust the hose evenly and lightly with a layer of flour.
6. Go outdoors (in the rain).
7. Quickly expose the nylon to the rain to capture several drops.
8. Go indoors.
9. Measure the diameter of three of the drops. Record these diameters on Figure 1-3.
10. See Figure 1-4 to calculate the volume of a drop.

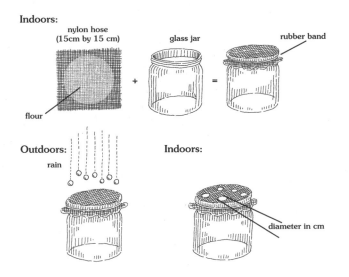

1–2 Lab Setup

Drop number	Diameter (cm)	Radius (cm)	Volume (cc=ml)
1			
2			
3			

1-3 Raindrop size data table

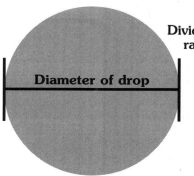

Divide the diameter by two to obtain the radius.

Volume of a sphere:

$$\frac{4}{3}\pi r^3 \text{ (in cm3)}$$

π equals approximately 3.14

1-4 Raindrop size calculations

GOING FURTHER

Obtain mineral oil or cooking oil. Pour 200 milliliters in a plastic see-through container. Now, "trap" several raindrops in this container. Describe the shapes of the drops as they strike the surface. Watch as the drops travel to the bottom of the container. What form does the droplet appear to take now?

• An inch of rain? Spread over one acre, this inch of water would weigh more than 200 thousand pounds. That's nearly 30 thousand gallons of water.

From the *World Almanac and Book of Facts*

QUESTION

1. What were the shapes of the impressions left by the raindrops after they struck the nylon hose? Why do you think were they shaped like this?

THE WIND CHILL FACTOR

Objective:

Observe a model that demonstrates evaporation and wind chill.

Materials:

- shallow pan
- water
- thermometer
- fan
- watch or clock with second hand
- graph paper
- pencil

When water evaporates, cooling takes place and temperature decreases. The opposite is true when condensation occurs. Condensation is a warming process, and heat is given off when gaseous water returns to the liquid phase. Here, you'll see a model of what happens to the temperature when wind blows across a body of water.

PROCEDURE

1. See Figure 1-1.
2. Place 3 centimeters of water in the pan.
3. Place the thermometer in the pan.
4. Make sure the bulb of the thermometer is partially submerged.
5. Record the beginning temperature on Figure 1-2.
6. Start the fan.
7. On Figure 1-2, record the temperature every minute until minute 10.
8. See Figure 1-3 for a sample graph of similarly recorded data.
9. Graph recorded data on graph paper using the appropriate scales.
10. See Figure 1-4 through 1-10 for wind chill charts to use for outside temperatures and wind speeds for both Fahrenheit and Celsius. You can obtain the wind speed from a radio broadcast.

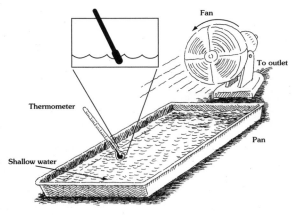

1–1 Wind chill setup

Minute	0	1	2	3	4	5	6	7	8	9	10
Temperature (degree C)											

1-2 Wind chill data table

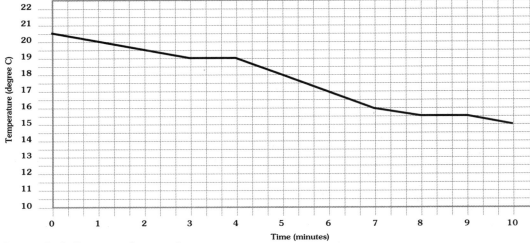

1-3 Wind chill example graph

Actual temperature (degree F)	Wind speed (miles per hour)							
	5	10	15	20	25	30	35	40
35	33	21	16	12	7	5	3	1
34	32	20	15	10	6	4	2	0
33	31	19	14	8	4	2	0	-1
32	29	18	13	7	3	1	-1	-2
31	28	17	12	5	1	-1	-3	-3
30	27	16	11	3	0	-2	-4	-4
29	26	15	9	2	-1	-4	-6	-6
28	25	13	7	0	-3	-6	-8	-8
27	23	12	5	-1	-4	-7	-9	-10
26	22	10	3	-3	-6	-9	-11	-13
25	21	9	1	-4	-7	-11	-13	-15
24	20	8	0	-5	-9	-12	-14	-16
23	19	6	-2	-6	-10	-14	-16	-18

Equivalent Temperature

1-4 Wind chill Fahrenheit chart 1

Actual temperature (degree F)	Wind speed (miles per hour)							
	5	10	15	20	25	30	35	40
-5	-11	-27	-40	-46	-52	-56	-60	-62
-6	-12	-28	-41	-47	-53	-57	-61	-63
-7	-13	-29	-42	-48	-54	-59	-63	-65
-8	-13	-29	-43	-50	-56	-60	-64	-66
-9	-14	-30	-44	-51	-57	-62	-66	-68
-10	-15	-31	-45	-52	-58	-63	-67	-69

Equivalent Temperature

1-7 Wind chill Fahrenheit chart 4

Actual temperature (degree C)	Wind speed (kilometers per hour)							
	Calm	10	20	30	40	50	60	70
-15	-15	-20	-29	-34	-38	-41	-42	-43
-20	-20	-25	-35	-42	-46	-48	-50	-51
-25	-25	-31	-42	-49	-53	-56	-58	-59
-30	-30	-37	-48	-56	-60	-64	-66	-67

Equivalent Temperature

1-9 Wind chill Celsius chart 2

Actual temperature (degree F)	Wind speed (miles per hour)							
	5	10	15	20	25	30	35	40
22	18	5	-3	-7	-12	-15	-17	-19
21	17	3	-5	-8	-13	-17	-19	-21
20	16	2	-6	-9	-15	-18	-20	-22
19	15	1	-7	-11	-16	-20	-21	-23
18	14	0	-8	-12	-18	-21	-23	-25
17	14	0	9	-14	-19	-23	-24	-26
16	13	-1	-10	-15	-21	-24	-26	-28
15	12	-2	-11	-17	-22	-26	-27	-29
14	11	-3	-12	-18	-23	-27	-29	-30
13	10	-5	-14	-20	-25	-29	-30	-32
12	9	-6	-15	-21	-26	-30	-32	-33
11	8	-8	-17	-23	-28	-32	-33	-35
10	7	-9	-18	-24	-29	-33	-35	-36

Equivalent Temperature

1-5 Wind chill Fahrenheit chart 2

Actual temperature (degree C)	Wind speed (kilometers per hour)							
	Calm	10	20	30	40	50	60	70
10	10	8	3	1	-1	-2	-3	-4
5	5	2	-3	-6	-8	-10	-11	-12
0	0	-3	-10	-13	-16	-18	-19	-20
-5	-5	-9	-16	-20	-23	-25	-27	-28
-10	-10	-14	-23	-27	-31	-33	-35	-35

Equivalent Temperature

1-8 Wind chill Celsius chart 1

Actual temperature (degree C)	Wind speed (kilometers per hour)							
	Calm	10	20	30	40	50	60	70
-35	-35	-42	-55	-63	-68	-71	-74	-75
-40	-40	-48	-61	-70	-75	-79	-82	-83
-45	-45	-53	-68	-77	-83	-87	-90	-91
-50	-50	-59	-74	-84	-90	-94	-97	-99

Equivalent Temperature

1-10 Wind chill Celsius chart 3

Actual temperature (degree F)	Wind speed (miles per hour)							
	5	10	15	20	25	30	35	40
9	6	-10	-19	-26	-31	-35	-37	-38
8	5	-11	-21	-27	-32	-36	-38	-40
7	3	-13	-22	-29	-34	-38	-40	-41
6	2	-14	-24	-30	-35	-39	-41	-43
5	1	-15	-25	-32	-37	-41	-43	-45
4	0	-16	-27	-34	-39	-43	-45	-48
3	-2	-18	-28	-35	-40	-44	-47	-49
2	-3	-19	-30	-37	-42	-46	-48	-50
1	-5	-21	-31	-38	-43	-47	-50	-52
0	-6	-22	-33	-40	-45	-49	-52	-54
-1	-7	-23	-34	-41	-46	-50	-54	-56
-2	-8	-24	-36	-42	-48	-52	-55	-57
-3	-9	-25	-37	-44	-49	-53	-57	-59
-4	-10	-26	-39	-45	-51	-55	-58	-60

Equivalent Temperature

1-6 Wind chill Fahrenheit chart 3

QUESTIONS

1. Did the temperature appear to drop steadily?
2. Was there any *plateau* (leveling off) in the temperature as it dropped?
3. At what minute did the temperature drop and remain at until the end of 10 minutes?
4. If hot water (instead of tap water) had been used, what would the results have been?
5. As you climb out of a pool on a warm day, you feel colder. Explain why this occurs in terms of evaporation.

igure 1-1 shows the "microweather" of saturated air surrounding a beaker. This is similar to a valley with trapped, moist air surrounded by hills. An early morning fog could eventually cover the region when this moist air cools.

Objective:

Calculate the *dew point* of air inside a container filled with ice. Dew point is the temperature at which water vapor in the air begins to condense.

Materials:

- one thermometer
- one 500-milliliter beaker
- ice

PROCEDURE

1. See Figure 1-2.
2. On Figure 1-3, record the temperature of the air just inside the opening of the empty 500-milliliter beaker.
3. Hold the thermometer just inside the opening of the beaker for the next two steps.
4. Fill the beaker with several ice cubes. Don't let the thermometer bulb touch the ice cubes. See Figure 1-4.
5. When drops of moisture appear on the outside of the container, record the temperature on Figure 1-3. This is the dew point.
6. See Figure 1-5 and 1-6 to calculate the relative humidity of the air above the ice cubes.

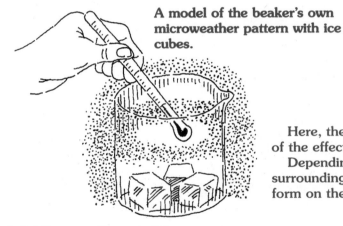

A model of the beaker's own microweather pattern with ice cubes.

Here, the spray pattern is a representation of the effects of the cold from the ice cubes. Depending on the amount of water vapor surrounding the beaker, condensation will form on the exterior of the glass surface.

1-1 Microweather model

Thermometer held by hand

Empty beaker—the thermometer must be held inside the dry beaker

1-2 Lab setup

Beaker with ice cubes—the thermometer must be held just inside the beaker, but above the ice. When condensation forms on the beaker's exterior, record that temperature.

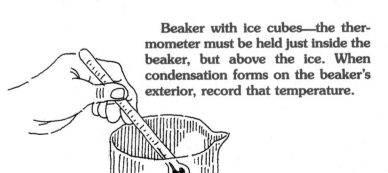

ice cubes

1-4 Beaker with cubes

Empty beaker temperature (degree C) A	Temperature when condensation forms (degree C) B	Difference in both readings (A-B)	Relative humidity (%)

1-3 Data table

Empty beaker temperature (degree C)	Temperature difference (degree C)									
	1	2	3	4	5	6	7	8	9	10
6	86	73	60	48	35	24	11			
8	87	75	63	51	40	29	19	8		
10	88	77	66	55	44	34	24	15	6	
12	89	78	68	58	48	39	29	21	12	
14	90	79	70	60	51	42	34	26	18	10
16	90	81	71	63	54	46	38	30	23	15
	Relative Humidity Around Beaker									

1–5 Humidity table 1

Empty beaker temperature (degree C)	Temperature difference (degree C)									
	1	2	3	4	5	6	7	8	9	10
18	91	82	73	65	57	49	41	34	27	20
20	91	83	74	66	59	51	44	38	31	24
22	92	83	76	68	61	54	47	41	34	28
24	92	84	77	69	62	56	49	44	37	31
26	92	85	78	71	64	58	51	47	40	34
28	93	85	78	72	65	59	53	48	42	37
	Relative Humidity Around Beaker									

1–6 Humidity table 2

QUESTIONS

1. Why did you have to wait for condensation to form?

2. When condensation formed, was the air around the beaker saturated?

Objective:
Observe a "collision" of cold and warm air, and the results of such a collision.

Materials:
- aquarium
- four sand bags, refrigerated for at least three hours
- one 500-milliliter beaker
- hot water
- plastic wrap or glass covering

 cold front is a shock wave of cool, dense air that slams into warm air, wedging it skyward. The warm air expands, cools, and condenses into a cloud formation called a *squall line.* The weather accompanying this squall line can be quite violent.

PROCEDURE

1. See Figure 1-1.
2. Be sure the sand bags have been in the refrigerator for at least three hours.
3. Place the sand bags in one corner of the aquarium.
4. Fill a 500-milliliter beaker with 400 milliliters of hot water. Be careful!
5. Place the beaker in the corner of the aquarium, opposite the sand bags.
6. Cover the aquarium with plastic wrap or a glass cover.
7. Watch what occurs. See Figures 1-2 through 1-4.

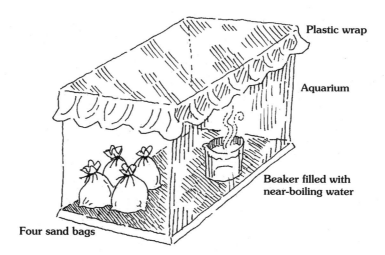

1-1 Lab setup

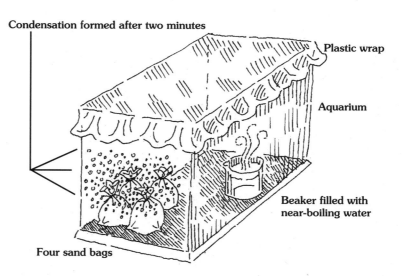

1-2 Example results

Note: clouds do not just "roll in." The moisture for each particular cloud is usually overhead. A front runs into these air "parcels" and pushes them upward, where they cool, condense, and then form into varying cloud types.

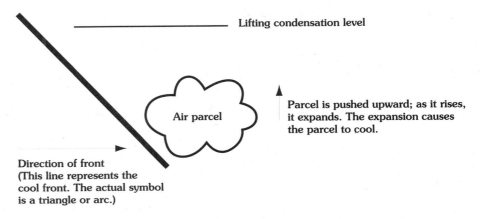

1-3 Cold front movement

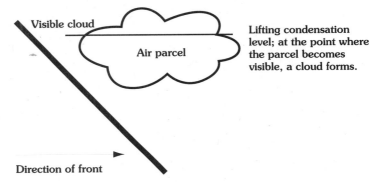

1-4 Cold front movement/cloud formation

QUESTIONS

1. Where was condensation forming in the aquarium?

2. Where did the evaporation occur in the aquarium?

COPYCAT PAGE SATELLITE NEWSPAPER PICTURES

Objective:
Observe cloud/weather patterns from newsprint pictures.

Materials:
- newspaper with weather satellite photos
- glue stick or tape
- scissors

n this experiment, it seems that the water should fall out of the glass. However, this is not so. Air in the atmosphere exerts a great deal of pressure—even in the classroom!

PROCEDURE

1. See Figure 1-1. Make copies as needed.
2. Use the daily newspaper map.
3. Cut the map out and tape or glue it to Figure 1-1.
4. Record the current weather conditions on Figure 1-1.
5. Keep a log for two weeks to observe changing weather patterns.
6. These maps could be placed on a plastic transparency for an overhead projector and used for the entire class.

DAY OF PICTURE: _____

DATE OF PICTURE: _____

NAME OF NEWSPAPER: _____

REGION OBSERVED (FROM NEWSPAPER PICTURE): _____

YOUR OUTSIDE WEATHER CONDITIONS (circle all that apply):

tornado	thunderstorm	hurricane	tropical storm	flood
hail	sleet	snow	rain	
fog	smog	smoke	haze	drizzle	marine layer
overcast	cloudy	partly sunny	partly cloudy	clear
windy	hot	cold	warm	cool

(Affix satellite photo here.)

1-1 Satellite photo page

FACTOIDS

- Hurricane Andrew, "the storm of the century," was the most expensive storm ever in U.S. history.
- Every acre of land on this planet has at least one molecule of dust from every other acre of land.

QUESTIONS

1. How far does a front (cold or warm) appear to move each day?
2. What direction do the fronts travel to and from, according to the satellite photos?
3. Is it possible for you to predict the weather conditions for your area based on the movement of the fronts observed in your pictures?

Naming the Clouds

Objective:

Introduce students to three basic cloud forms

Make a list of words on the board that could be used to describe the shapes of clouds. Students might suggest cotton balls, cauliflower, blanket, cotton candy, horsetail, etc.

Make a diagram of the three basic cloud shapes.

Then, ask students to copy the words onto a sheet of paper, using columns to form three groups. Ask them to group the words according to similar forms. For example, the words blanket, layer, and frosting might all be put together because they all describe flattened cloud shapes. Similarly, the words cotton balls, cauliflower, and mashed potatoes might all be grouped together because they all describe "heaped" or "puffy" cloud shapes.

Next, have students share the results of their work and allow students to come to the realization that clouds can be categorized as flat layers (stratus), heaped or puffy (cumulus), and thin and wispy (cirrus). You might also ask students the following questions:

- Why do scientists need to have names for clouds? (Scientists need names for clouds so they can communicate with each other about what kinds of clouds are in the sky and how clouds change and grow.)

- The words *stratus, cumulus,* and *cirrus* all come from a language called Latin. Why would scientists want to use Latin words to describe clouds? (Latin is a language that is used for scientific names for plants and animals. Latin names can be used and understood by scientists from around the world, even if their usual language is French, German, Spanish, or Chinese.)

- Who is the person who first suggested using these Latin names to describe clouds? (The person is Luke Howard, and Englishman who lived from 1772-1864.)

At the conclusion of the discussion, have students read *The Man Who Named the Clouds.* Then, give students each a sheet of drawing paper. Have them divide the paper into three parts and write one of the following words in each section: cirrus, stratus, or cumulus. Then, using paints, markers, crayons, cut paper, or colored pencils, have them draw the correct cloud form in each of the sections.

THE MAN WHO NAMED THE CLOUDS

Luke Howard (1772-1864) has been called the father of meteorology and the godfather of the clouds. He's the author of the first textbook on meteorology. His book, *The Climate of London,* is the first scientific study of urban climatology. However, Howard's most important contribution to the scientific study of weather is the system of cloud classification he devised.

Before Howard proposed his classification system, clouds were usually considered little more than ornaments in the sky—worthy of the attention of painters and poets, but not serious scientific study. Besides naming the clouds, Howard also proposed that clouds were a useful topic of research and a way of learning more about weather.

Little is known of Howard's early life or exactly when or how he devised his ideas about clouds and naming them. He was born in London on November 11, 1772. Historians believe that Howard may first have become interested in observing weather in 1783, when the eruption of the Japanese volcano Asamayama caused spectacular sunsets and displays in the sky around the world. Later in his life, Howard wrote that he had been interested in the sky and the study of weather from his boyhood, and that he had spent a great deal of time making and recording barometric measurements.

Howard attended school from 1780-86, where he later said he learned "too much Latin grammar and too little of anything else." After finishing school, he was apprenticed to a pharmacist. In his spare time, he studied French, chemistry, and botany.

When Howard finished his apprenticeship, he returned to London and found work as a wholesale druggist. But an accident at work in the lab almost proved to be fatal.

Howard fell from a ladder with a bottle of arsenic that he was holding in his hand. The broken bottle cut him deeply on the arm and the poison went directly into Howard's blood. For several days, Howard had severe bleeding, and the doctor who was treating him didn't really know how to help other than to bind the wound. Eventually, the wound did heal, but while Howard was disabled he continued his interests in learning about nature—especially the microscopic study of pollen. These studies probably contributed to his knowledge of scientific classification and ideas about categorizing clouds.

In 1796, a small group of London professional men decided to form a group for "stimulation and enlightenment on scientific matters." They named themselves the Askesian Society. Meetings were held every two weeks at the homes of various members. The members took turns proposing topics for scientific study, writing papers on the topics, and presenting the papers to members of the group. Papers that the group considered exceptional were recommended for publication.

Howard presented a number of papers during the time he was a member of this group. His essay *On the Modification of Clouds,* presented to the group one evening during the winter of 1802-03, described his ideas for classifying clouds and provided Latin names for various types of clouds.

Howard's original classification system named three distinct types of clouds: cirrus, cumulus, and stratus. According to Howard, cirrus clouds are the "highest and lightest" clouds. Cumulus clouds are "detached and hemispherical." And stratus clouds are associated with "mist and fog." Howard also described and named intermediate forms of clouds, such as cirrocumulus, cirrostratus, and cumulostratus. In addition, he proposed the word "nimbus" for rain clouds.

The ideas Howard proposed were apparently well received by the other members of the Askesian Society, because his essay was published in *Tilloch's Philosophical Magazine* in 1803. Howard's close friend, Silvanus Bevan, created etchings of various types of clouds to illustrate the essay. The essay was also printed in various other magazines and journals.

Several years later, the German poet Goethe discovered Howard's ideas. Goethe had been fascinated by the shape and form of clouds, and he praised Howard for "bestowing form on the formless . . ." In fact, Goethe was so excited by Howard's ideas that he wrote about them in poems entitled "Cirrus," "Nimbus," "Stratus," "Cumulus," and "To the Honoured Memory of Howard."

Luke Howard wasn't the only person trying to find a way to describe and categorize clouds during the this time. In fact, the year before Howard published his essay, the French naturalist Lamarck proposed a way of naming and classifying clouds. Lamarck's system didn't attract much attention, however, even in France. Howard's use of Latin names for the cloud types was probably one reason for widespread acceptance of his system, because Latin was the common language used by scientists of the time.

Howard's system for naming clouds came at an important time in the study of meteorology. In some ways, the study of meteorology had lagged behind the studies of other physical sciences. In the years between 1800 and 1820, however, scientists were making important discoveries about the atmosphere. Pioneering balloon flights were giving scientists the chance to make measurements of the air they had never been able to make before. Scientists were also beginning to realize the importance of ascending air currents to understanding weather and how certain types of clouds form. Howard's system of classifying clouds eventually became the basis for a common language atmospheric scientists could use to describe what was happening in the sky.

Luke Howard maintained his interest in weather and the sky throughout his entire life. His granddaughter described him as "a sensitive, delicate man, with a good deal of the oddity of genius." She remembers him as a person who would often stand beside the window, looking at the sky with a dreamy look—and occasionally calling everyone over to point out an unusual cloud and to describe its form. Almost two hundred years after Howard first proposed his system for naming clouds, scientists still look at the sky. They use the words *cirrus, cumulus,* and *stratus* to talk about what they see overhead—the words proposed by Luke Howard, the man who named the clouds.

Depending on the Weather

Did you know that 70% of all the earth is covered by ocean? These great expanses of water have a strong effect on the weather throughout the world. Most people might expect Alaska to have the coldest and most severe weather of all the United States. However, because of proximity to the ocean, Juneau has warmer, milder weather than Minnesota for 10 months of the year. People who live near ocean coasts have temperature swings of about 20 degrees throughout the year. People who live near the center of the continent can have temperature variances of up to 105 degrees. The difference is mainly because of the volume of water involved. The ocean takes a long time to cool down and to heat up. When the weather turns cold, the warmth of the ocean water generates heat into the air. When the air temperature turns hot, the coolness of the ocean keeps the air near the coast cool.

But the oceans affect more than just temperature. The Gulf Stream and other ocean currents moving up and down the coast can cause tropical storms, moisture in the form of rain and snow, and droughts when no moisture is generated. These currents bring cold or warm water from one area to another. Without warm currents from the tropics, the sea around Scandinavia and Great Britain would freeze!

Large tropical storms, or hurricanes, cause more deaths than any other type of storm. They begin as small storm cells over the ocean. The storms group together to form a swirl of cloud, moving westward across the ocean. Encouraged by strong winds high in the atmosphere, they draw in warm moist air, spinning tighter and tighter, leaving a low pressure spot in the middle called the eye. The rain and wind are at their worst next to the eye. Once the hurricane passes over land or moves over cooler water, the storm begins to die.

ACTIVITIES / DISCUSSION

1. How dependent are people on knowing about weather? When would it be critical for you to know what the weather will be like? Using fluent thinking, have students list as many jobs as they can for which knowing the weather is critical (e.g., farming, fishing, forestry, power industry, transportation, tourism, services like education, health, etc.). Identify why it would be important for people in these jobs to know about weather conditions—for example, life and death situations, economic issues, safety, people's comfort, etc.

2. Identify major cities located on the coasts and the interior of the United States—such as San Francisco, Juneau, Boston, Charleston, New Orleans, Kansas City, etc.—and other countries. For two to three months, collect their daily temperatures from the weather channel or the newspaper. Graph temperatures for each day. Are temperatures on either side of the continent similar? Explain how swings compare. How do temperature swings in the interior compare? Does it matter whether or not the city is in the northern or southern part of the continent? What factors make it hard to accurately predict the weather? Would it be easier to predict the weather on the coasts or in the interior of the continent? Why?

Center for Global Environmental Education
Hamline University
1536 Hewitt Avenue
St. Paul, MN 55104-1248
phone: 612-523-2480
e-mail:cgee@gw.hamline.edu
Web site: cgee.hamline.edu

FORECASTING THE WEATHER

The sun sets behind a gray curtain of clouds, replaced by a dim moon with a circle around it. The television meteorologist is saying that heavy snow will be flying by morning and school will most likely be cancelled for the day. How is a weather forecast like this one made, and will it be right?

People have tried to forecast the weather for thousands of years. The Bible, for instance, tells us that "in the evening you say there will be fair weather for the skies are red, and in the morning you say there will be foul weather for the skies are red and lowering." Sayings like this one are called weather proverbs or weather folklore, and were the way forecasts were made until about the 1800s.

By that time, instruments had been developed that measured the weather, and these observations showed how weather systems moved. Observations allowed better forecasts. More recently, starting in 1950, computers have been used to predict the weather. Computers help give forecasts that are more accurate than ever.

Although the way forecasts are made has changed through history, all of the different methods can still be helpful to us today when we try to forecast the weather. Let's take a look at ways to forecast the weather using three different tools: weather folklore, weather observations, and computers.

Weather Folklore

Long ago, people had to pay attention to nature's clues to forecast what might happen with the weather. For instance, in much of the world, weather moves from west to east. A shepherd seeing dark skies in the west knew rain was likely. A farmer seeing dark clouds in the east could guess the clouds were moving away.

Clues like these ended up being written down and taught to people as weather proverbs or folklore. The words were often put into simple sayings or poems that could be easily remembered. Proverbs based on what people saw in the sky were usually pretty good forecasting tools. Some of these include:

- "Red sky at night, sailor's delight; red sky in morning, sailors take warning"
- "Short notice, soon past; long notice, long past"
- "The moon with a circle brings water in her beak"

We now can use science to explain why these proverbs work. For instance, red skies usually happen around sunrise or sunset when the sun is low in the sky and shining on clouds. If the red skies happen at sunset, the sun is shining through clear skies to the west. Since weather moves from west to east, the clear skies will probably move over and give sunny weather the next day.

If the red skies occur in the morning, clear skies must be in the east, and the clouds in the west. The clouds and maybe rain or snow would probably move in during the day.

The second proverb works because weather that happens fast, like a thunderstorm, is usually small and ends quickly. Large weather systems that cover big areas with rain or snow start with thin clouds that very slowly dim the sun or moon and get thicker over many hours. Sometimes the rain or snow may take more than a day to begin after the clouds first come. These weather systems give lots of clues that they are coming, and because they are so big, rain or snow will fall for a long time.

In the last proverb, the circle refers to a ring or halo that can be seen around the moon or sun. These circles form when a thin layer of clouds made of tiny ice crystals like snowflakes covers the sky. When sun or moonlight shines through the ice crystals, it bends (refracts) in the same way it would through a prism or through raindrops creating a rainbow, and the bent light forms a whitish ring around the moon or sun. Since thin clouds are usually the first sign that a large storm is coming, a ring around the moon or sun is a good clue that bad weather is coming.

Because people like to know what the weather will do in the next season, and not just the next day, some folklore tries to predict the weather far into the future. This folklore usually relates the weather to plants and animals. One proverb says that animals will grow longer fur if a very cold, snowy winter is coming. Another says that trees will produce more nuts if the winter is going to be bad. Unfortunately, these proverbs don't seem to be true (Nut production is related to the amount of rain that fell during the spring and summer.)

Another popular proverb says that the furry, black and brown-striped woolly bear caterpillar can be used to predict winter weather. The blacker the caterpillars are, the worse the winter will be. Scientists now believe that the stripes depend on who the mother and father caterpillar are and not on the weather!

Thus, weather folklore that uses the sky can help predict weather, but folklore that uses animals or plants usually cannot. Even folklore that doesn't forecast the weather has some value, though, because it makes us pay attention to the animals and plants around us.

Weather Observations

Weather proverbs are really one type of weather observation, made with the instruments of our own senses—sight, sound, smell. Weather can be very complicated, however, and to forecast it better, we need observations from other instruments. By the 1800s, people had invented good instruments to measure the temperature, pressure, moisture, and wind in the atmosphere.

A thermometer measures temperature by using a material that gets bigger or smaller as the air gets warmer or colder. Most thermometers have a liquid in them called mercury, which gets bigger as it gets hotter.

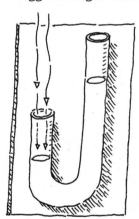

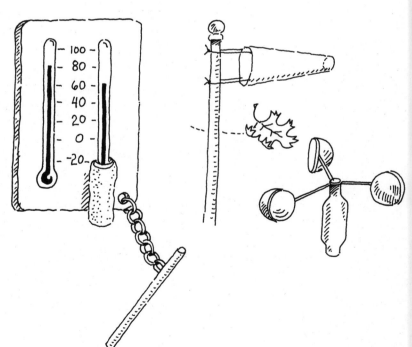

Figure 1
Typical weather instruments (from left to right: thermometer for temperature, barometer for pressure, sling psychrometer for humidity, and wind sock and anemometer for wind direction and speed).

The speed at which molecules in a given space of air are moving determines the pressure the air exerts on everything it touches. Air pressure is measured by a *barometer*. Air pressure is very helpful in forecasting the weather, since low pressure usually has rain or snow near it, and high pressure usually brings fair weather.

The amount of rain or snow that falls from the sky is related to the moisture in it, or its relative humidity. A *psychrometer* or *hygrometer* is used to measure this moisture in the air. Some people complain that their hair gets frizzy when the air is humid. Hair expands when humidity is high, and thus some hygrometers use hair to measure humidity.

Wind vanes or wind socks tell us the direction of the wind, and *anemometers* tell us the wind speed. Wind measurements can help predict the weather because winds move warm and cold, and wet and dry, air from one place to another.

Although having these measurements at one spot can help a little in weather forecasting, having many measurements all over the country or world is more useful.

In the 1800s, when telegraphs were invented and trains started carrying people on cross-country trips, the United States government decided it would be good to know what the weather was doing *everywhere* the trains traveled. The National Weather Service was created to take these weather measurements. Telegraphs were used to communicate all the measurements to one place so that they could be written down on maps.

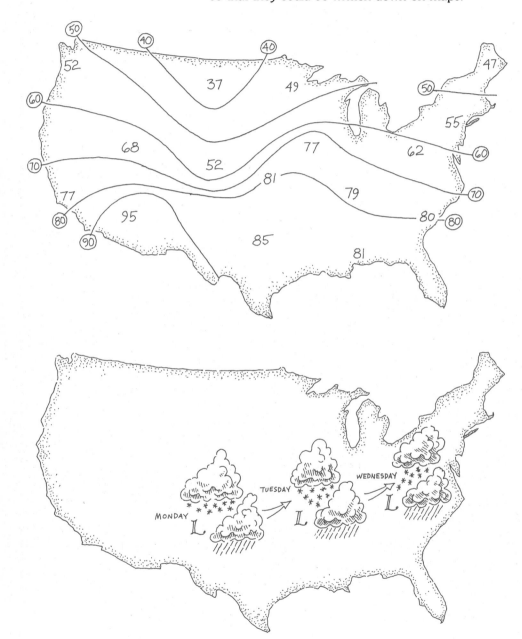

When weather measurements are gathered and recorded on a weather map, they can be studied to figure out what the atmosphere is doing. Forecasters can draw lines of temperature on maps to show where it is warm and where it is cold. The process of drawing on weather maps is called *analysis*.

When analysis is done at many different times, it shows how weather is moving. After a few years of weather observations, scientists discovered that storms often traveled along similar paths, called *storm tracks*. When instruments were put onto weather balloons which carried them up to take measurements at high levels in the atmosphere, the measurements showed that strong winds blow about 7 miles up in the atmosphere. Scientists called the winds the *jet stream,* and found that storms often followed the jet stream.

Scientists also found that storms followed a pattern in the way they changed as they moved. Using these facts, they were able to make better weather forecasts than weather folklore. For instance, weather systems grow when they are located in an area with big temperature changes. If it is very cold to your north and very warm to your south and a small area of rain is nearby, you should expect a bigger area of rain to form as the weather system moves eastward. Thus, weather observations are helpful in weather forecasting.

Figure 3
A weather system's movement in previous days can help predict where it will move in the future.

Computer Forecasts

By observing the weather with lots of instruments in lots of places, we can see how weather systems normally move—and change as they move. However, nature likes to surprise us, and no two weather systems are ever exactly alike, just like snowflakes. Thus, if our only tool to predict the weather is observation, our forecasts will always be a little wrong since each weather event will behave a little differently from any other.

Fortunately, the atmosphere is a fluid like water, and we therefore have a fairly good idea of how it will behave when different forces act on it. Just as gravity pulls you to the ground when you jump from a chair, gravity also tries to pull the air toward the ground. Just as a fire adds heat to the air around it and warms it, the earth, warmed by the sun, warms the air above it.

Because we know the forces that can change the atmosphere, we can write equations that tell us how weather will change over time. These scientific equations are complicated, though, and would be impossible to solve in our heads.

Computers, though, take complicated equations written into programs and solve them very quickly. Because of this, computers are a very helpful tool for improving weather forecasting. The weather observations made with thermometers and barometers can be fed to computers, and the computers can then predict with a fair degree of accuracy how the weather will change in the future. In the United States, computer forecasts are made several times a day at the National Center for Environmental Prediction.

Computers allow us to better figure out how a storm will change as it moves, since the computer programs use the scientific equations. Because of this, weather forecasts have improved so much that a forecast today for the next two days is more accurate than a one-day forecast made in the 1970s. If computers can do such good jobs with the weather equations, why are many weather forecasts still wrong?

One reason is that weather measurements are only taken at selected cities across the world. This means there are large areas like oceans where no measurements are taken, and we therefore don't know what the weather is doing there. Without those measurements, the computer doesn't know everything there is to know. Weather involves so many tug-of-wars in the atmosphere that it has been said a butterfly flapping its wings in a faraway jungle can produce a snowstorm in the United States weeks later. Until we measure every "butterfly" in the atmosphere, computer forecasts may be wrong because we miss some small but important weather detail.

In addition, computer equations that predict what happens inside a thunderstorm, or other complicated weather features, are not perfect because we still don't know everything that goes on in nature. We can only make our computer forecasting programs as good as our understanding of nature.

Computers not only help predict the weather by running forecasting programs, but they also allow us to use new weather instruments that take millions of measurements. We could never keep all the measurements organized without computers. These new inventions include satellites and weather radar. These tools help us to "fill in the blanks" over oceans and other sparsely populated areas. The observations made with these machines help us to make better forecasts for small weather systems that might affect us in the next few hours.

Figure 4
The atmosphere is affected by lots of scientific processes that can be put into equations and programmed into computers to help predict the weather.

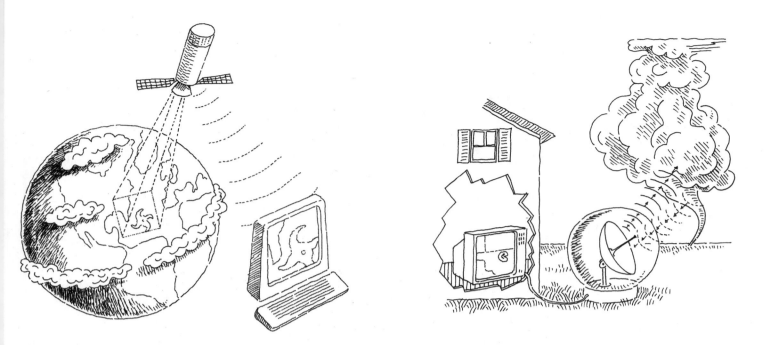

Figure 5
Above left: Satellites take pictures of the Earth from outer space, letting us see where clouds are.

Figure 6
Above right: Weather radar bounces energy off of precipitation so that we can see how bad the weather is, even if storms are far away.

Satellites are like eyes in outer space that take pictures of our planet, showing where clouds are. Some satellites have eyes that can see in the dark. These infrared satellites give us pictures during the night when ordinary cameras would see only black. Thanks to satellites, we can see dangerous hurricanes when they are still far out in the ocean, away from any land or ships to report them. Because they can't hide from us, we can better predict hurricane movement and give better warnings to people. Some hurricanes used to kill thousands of people. Now, even the worst ones rarely harm people who listen to the warnings.

The most helpful invention for warning us of tornadoes was invented as an accident! Weather radar was born when people in World War II noticed that precipitation got in the way when they were trying to locate enemy planes on radar. Although few people back then were happy when rain or snow blocked a view of an enemy plane, radar later became an excellent way for forecasters to see where precipitation was falling. A weather radar first sends out energy and then measures how much energy bounces back to it from raindrops or snowflakes. Usually the more energy bounced back, the heavier the precipitation.

One type of radar, *Doppler,* not only shows us precipitation, but also shows how fast air is moving. Doppler radar works like police radar guns, but instead of figuring out who is speeding, the radar tells us what the winds are doing inside clouds. Doppler radar can see when the air inside a thunderstorm begins to spin. Once the spinning gets faster, a storm can produce a violent tornado.

As recently as the 1980s, most forecasters couldn't warn people of a tornado until it had already touched the ground and someone could call the weather station. Now, most tornadoes can be seen by radar before anyone on the ground sees them, and warnings can be given 10, 20 or even 30 minutes ahead of time. Most of the United States is now watched by Doppler radars called NEXRADs.

Conclusion

Having learned a lot about our atmosphere over the last few hundred years, we now make weather forecasts that are more accurate than ever before. Although computers and new ways of observing the weather have been a huge help, the best weather forecasts are made by taking what the computer says and making some changes based on the old-fashioned ways of forecasting. No matter whether it be the weather proverbs from thousands of years ago or satellites in outer space today, all things that help forecast the weather depend on knowing what nature is doing. Whenever you are outside, take time to watch the sky. You may not have a powerful computer sitting in your bedroom, but you might surprise yourself at how well you can forecast the weather just by paying attention to the world around you.

Follow the Weather

Since one way to forecast the weather is simply to assume that one type of weather will move from one place to another, weather forecasters need to be good at geography. This game will help students learn the relationships between geographical places, while at the same time showing them how this method of forecasting works. Remember that weather systems can change as they move, so this method of forecasting won't be entirely accurate. But it can give you a pretty good idea of the kinds of weather changes that are likely.

First, cut out the weather clues below and put them into a hat. Divide your students into four or five teams. Have someone from the first team draw a clue from the hat and read it to the entire group. After the team hears the clue they have one minute to predict the weather for the city or state requested on the piece of paper. (To accurately predict the weather, students will have to know where the places are that are mentioned in the clue.) After one minute, the team member who drew the clue has thirty seconds to post the clue on the map at the location for which the forecast was made. (To simplify the game, cities can be ignored and you can use only states or countries.) Score ten points for a correct forecast and five extra points for correct placement of the clue on the map.

Only team one has an opportunity to answer the forecast question (since most questions have yes or no answers). However, if team one misses locating the city or state on the map, team two can earn one less point (four) if they can locate the place. Allow each team to have an opportunity to find the place, lowering the point value by one point each time, until the city or state is located, or the point value becomes zero.

- It snowed last night in Salt Lake City, Utah and the snowstorm is moving east. Will it snow today in Denver, Colorado from this storm?

- It rained yesterday in Dallas, Texas, and the rain moved to Little Rock, Arkansas last night. Is it likely that rainstorm will be in Houston, Texas today?

- It is now thundering with lots of lightning in Philadelphia, Pennsylvania. The thunderstorm was in Washington, D.C. 4 hours ago. Do you think New York City will see a thunderstorm in the next couple of hours?

- People in Seattle, Washington used umbrellas yesterday. The rain there was moving northeast. Is it likely you will need an umbrella today if you live in Boise, Idaho?

- It was very hot yesterday in Nashville, Tennessee. The hot air is moving north. Do you think it will be hot today in South Bend, Indiana?

- Schools closed down at 10:00 o'clock in the morning in Bismark, North Dakota because a blizzard hit. Two hours later, the same thing happened in Jamestown, North Dakota which is about 100 miles east of Bismark. Is it likely the blizzard will hit Fargo, North Dakota before school is done at 3:00 o'clock?

- It was sunny two days ago in Louisiana, but raining in Texas. It was sunny yesterday in Mississippi, but raining in Louisiana. Is it likely to be sunny today in Mississippi?

- It is a snowy day in Nebraska today. The snow is moving east. Is it likely to be snowy tomorrow in Iowa?

- A hurricane hit land last night in North Carolina and it is moving northwest. Is it likely the weather will be nice today in Virginia?

- It was record cold this morning in Kentucky, and the cold air is moving southeast. Would there more likely be cold weather or warm weather tomorrow in South Carolina?

- A few hours ago, it became very windy in Los Angeles, California. The winds are moving east. Will you get to fly your kite soon in Reno, Nevada?

- Every part of the United States west of the Mississippi River was sunny yesterday. Will it likely be cloudy or sunny today in St. Louis, Missouri, if the weather systems are moving from west to east?

- A hurricane hit Puerto Rico yesterday, and was moving west. Will the hurricane hit Brazil soon?

- On Sunday, it rained in Spain. On Monday, it rained in France. Will it rain on Tuesday in Denmark?

- The only thunderstorms today in Africa occurred in Ghana. They were moving west. Will people in Sudan probably see those storms tomorrow?

- If it is raining in China today, and the rainstorm is moving northeast, what kind of weather would you forecast tomorrow for Korea?

- It was very cold last night in Argentina, but very warm in Chile. The weather is moving north. Will it be cold or warm in the next few days in Bolivia?

- A dust storm stirred up the desert sands in Egypt yesterday. The dust was blowing northeast. Will it be easy to stay clean today in Israel?

What Was the Weather Like?

Objectives:
Learn how weather observations are taken, and observe trends in the weather.

Ages:
Primary, Intermediate, Advanced

Materials:
- thermometer
- barometer
- wind vane or wind sock
- anemometer
- notebook

Subjects:
Science and Math

Have students keep a weather diary. Locate a thermometer, barometer, and possibly a wind vane or wind sock and anemometer. Better still, make your own with the class. Have students take turns reading the instruments and recording the observations. They can also look at the sky and choose the amount of cloud cover to record. Clear means there are almost no clouds; scattered means less than half of the sky covered in clouds; broken means one-half to three-quarters cloud coverage; and overcast indicates completely cloudy or nearly so. Have students record rain, snow, or thunderstorms, also. In addition, if a rain guage is available, allow students to record precipitation amounts. Snow is usually measured with a ruler, and melted down to yield a liquid amount.

Take observations several times each day for a period of at least one week. Be sure to write down the time of each observation. Then have students look at the diary to look for weather trends. Have them notice at which time each day it is usually coldest outside and which time is usually warmest. See if one part of the day is cloudier than another. Have them describe how the weather changed leading up to any precipitation.

If time permits and the diary can be maintained for a longer time period like a month, explore climatology with the students by figuring out the average temperatures each day or for each observation time during the month. Total precipitation or snowfall can also be determined.

Running a Weather Radar

Objective:
Demonstrate some basic principles used in weather radars.

Ages:
Primary

Materials:
- whistle or other noise-maker
- ordinary classroom objects of different sizes

Subject:
Science

Help young students understand how weather radar works and the difference between old radars that measure reflectivity, or intensity of precipitation, and newer Doppler radars that also measure winds.

Choose several students to represent rain shows or snow showers. Have them stand at different distances from one side of the room. Allow other students to be the radar pulse of energy that leaves the radar and reflects off of the rain or snow particles. Have the student who is the radar pulse run and tag a rain or snow shower and return to the radar site. Use a stopwatch if possible and record the amount of time for the radar pulse to return. Repeat using different showers that are located at different distances. Show the students that it takes longer for the pulse to return if the precipitation is farther away, and explain that this is how the radar knows where the precipitation is located.

Vary this technique by having the rain and snow shower students hold objects of different sizes, where the size of the object represents the intensity of the precipitation. Let the radar pulse students carry the object back to the radar as they make their journey. This represents the amount of power that the radar sees. Explain that big objects would show up as an intense radar echo, and would indicate weather like a thunderstorm. Light objects would show up as a weak radar echo, and would indicate light rain or a gentle snowfall.

Finally, demonstrate how Doppler radar works by having a student (or teacher) run across the room blowing a whistle or using another noise maker. Let the students describe how the sound changes as the noise approaches and then moves away. Ask them when the pitch sounded higher or lower. Relate the pitch to approaching or receding movement.

Next, have the students close their eyes, and repeat the experiment. Ask them to determine which path the noise took this time. Explain that this is how Doppler radar measures the wind speeds in a storm.

A Vote for Forecasting

Objective:
Discuss how people feel about weather forecasting

Ages:
Intermediate and Advanced

Materials:
- paper
- pencils and pens

Subject:
Language Arts, Math, and Science

Have students conduct polls of neighbors and friends regarding weather forecasting. Let them choose questions that will show the option of the public toward the accuracy of weather forecasts. Allow students to include questions that they think of themselves. Good questions might include:

- Do you feel that weather forecasts are usually correct or incorrect?
- Do you think weather forecasts are more accurate now than they were ten years ago?
- What is your favorite kind of weather?
- Have you ever planned an outside activity when the forecast was good, but then had it rain or snow?
- Do you think forecasters do a better job of predicting snow, or predicting rain?

- Have you ever taken shelter in a tornado warning?
- Has a weather forecast ever caused you to change your plans?
- How do you think weather forecasts are made?
- Do you know of any weather folklore?

Bibliography

Note: A * at the end of a listing indicates that the book is a good source of weather pictures.

REFERENCE BOOKS

The American Weather Book by David M. Ludlum (American Meteorological Society, 1989). A month-by-month look at noteworthy weather events.

Calculating the Weather by Frederik Nebeker (Academic Press, 1995)

Eric Sloane's Almanac and Weather Folklore by Eric Sloane (Hawthorne Books, Inc., 1955)

A Field Guide to the Atmosphere (a Peterson Guide) by Vincent J. Schaffer and John A. Day (Houghton Mifflin, 1983)

From Weathervanes to Satellites: An Introduction to Meteorology by Herbert Spiegel and Arnold Gruber (Books on Demand, 1983)

Glossary of Weather and Climate edited by Ira W. Geer (American Meteorological Society, 1996)

Meteorology Today, 3rd ed., by C. Donald Ahrens (West, 1988)

1001 Questions Answered about the Weather by Frank H. Forrester (Dover, 1982)

Practical Weather Forecasting by Frank Mitchell-Christie (Barron's, 1978).

The USA Today Weather Almanac by Jack Williams (Random House, 1995)

The USA Today Weather Book by Jack Williams (Random House, 1992)*

Weather by Paul Lehr (Golden Guide, Western Publishing, 1987)

The Weather Almanac, 6th ed., edited by James A. Ruffner and Frank E. Blair (Gale Research, 1991)

The Weather Companion: An Album of Meteorological History, Science, Legend, and Folklore by Gary Lockhart (Wiley, 1988)

The Weather Factor by David M. Ludlum (Houghton Mifflin, 1984)

Weather Spotter's Guide by F. Wilson and F. Mansfield (EDC, 1995)*

Weather Wisdom: Facts & Folklore of Weather Forecasting by Albert Lee (Congdon & Weed, 1990)

Weather Wisdom—Proverbs, Superstitions, and Signs, compiled by Stewart A. Kingsbury, Mildred E. Kingsbury, and Wolfgang Mieder (Peter Lang, 1996)

Weather Wizard's Cloud Book by Louis D. Rubin, Sr. and Jim Duncan (Algonquin Books, 1984)

CHILDREN'S BOOKS

The Cloud Book by Tomie DePaola (Holiday House, 1975), Primary and Intermediate*

Cloudy with a Chance of Meatballs by Judith Barrett (Simon & Schuster, 1982). Fantasy—weather brings food from the sky. Primary

A January Fog Will Freeze a Hog and Other Weather Folklore compiled and edited by Hubert Davis (Crown, 1977), Intermediate

Hurricane Watch by Franklyn Branley (HarperCollins Children's Books, 1985), Intermediate

Look at Weather by Rena K. Kirkpatrick (Raintree, 1985), Primary

The Magic School Bus inside a Hurricane by Joanna Cole (Scholastic, 1995), Primary and Intermediate

Mouse and Mole and the All-Weather Train Ride by Doug Cushman (W. H. Freeman and Company, 1995), Primary

Our Violent Earth by Nancy Watson et al. (National Geographic, 1982), Intermediate and Advanced*

A Peterson First Guide to Clouds and Weather by John A. Day and Vincent J. Schaefer (Houghton Mifflin, 1991)

Rain and Hail by Franklyn Branley (HarperCollins Children's Books, 1983), Primary and Intermediate

Snow is Falling by Franklyn Branley (HarperCollins Children's Books, 1986), Primary

The Stickybear Book of Weather by Richard Hefter (Optimum Resource, 1983), Primary*

Tornado Alert by Franklyn Branley (HarperCollins Children's Books, 1988), Primary and Intermediate

Weather, edited by David Ellyard (Time-Life, 1996), Advanced

Weather by Tom Keirein (National Geographic, 1994), All ages.

The Weather (a Let's Investigate Science book) by Robin Kerrod (Marshall Cavendish, 1994), Advanced

Weather Forecasting by Gail Gibbons (Simon & Schuster Children's, 1993), Primary and Intermediate

Weather: Mind-Boggling Experiments You Can Turn Into Science Fair Projects (a Spectacular Science Project book) by Janice VanCleave (Wiley, 1995), Intermediate and Advanced

Weather Watch! by Julian Rowe and Molly Perham (Childrens, 1994), Primary

Weatherwatch by Valerie Wyatt (Addison-Wesley, 1990), Intermediate and Advanced

Weather Words and What They Mean by Gail Gibbons (Holiday House, 1990), Primary

When a Storm Comes Up by Allan Fowler (Children's Press, 1995), Primary*

Why Does Lightning Strike? by Terry Martin (Dorling Kindersley, 1996), Primary

Wind and Weather (a Voyages of Discovery book)(Scholastic, 1994), Intermediate*

OTHER PUBLICATIONS AND POSTERS

The American Weather Observer—Monthly climatology newsletter to serve all those who have a fascination with weather. Written for the layperson and including photos, statistics, how-to information, personal weather experiences, and numerous other regular features, the publication also supports the mission of the American Weather Observer Supplemental Observation Network (American Weather Observer, P.O. Box 455, Belvidere, IL 61008-0455 for free sample).

Weather Nature Finder (Intermediate and Advanced)—Identification wheel with weather facts and pictures of a dozen types of clouds and other weather phenomena (Hubbard Scientific/American Educational Products, Inc., 401 Hickory St., P.O. Box 2121, Ft. Collins, CO 80522).

Weatherwise—Bimonthly magazine written for the layperson (Weatherwise, Heldref Publications, 1319 18th St. NW, Washington, DC 20036).
World Wide Weather (Advanced)—Poster (National Science Teachers Association, 1840 Wilson Blvd., Arlington, VA 22201-3000).

VIDEOS, FILMSTRIPS, AND SLIDES

Bringing the Rain to Kapiti Plain features a legend about bringing rain to the African plains, and *Come a Tide* describes floods, hurricanes, and other severe weather. Both are Reading Rainbow videos (Primary) that interview scientists who study the weather (GPN, P.O. Box 80669, Lincoln, NE 68501-0669)
Discovering Our Earth's Atmosphere (Advanced)—Video with teacher's guide. *Unusual Atmospheric Phenomena and Cloud Types*—Slide sets (American Educational Products, P.O. Box 2121, Ft. Collins, CO 80522)
National Weather Service—Slide sets to lend on weather-related topics (NOAA/National Weather Service, Customer Service, 1325 East-West Highway, Room 14370, Silver Spring, MD 20910)
Telling the Weather (Intermediate) and *Weather: Come Rain, Come Shine* (Advanced)—Videos. *An Introduction to Weather* (Intermediate and Advanced)—Three filmstrips on "Weather & the Water Cycle," "Observing Changes in Weather," and "Measuring & Forecasting Weather." *Watching the Weather* (Primary)—Two filmstrips on "What Makes the Weather?" and "Observing Weather" (National Geographic Society, Educational Services, P.O. Box 98019, Washington, DC 20090-8019)
Weather-related videos (Karol Media, 350 N. Pennsylvania Ave., P.O. Box 7600, Wilkes-Barre, PA 18773-7600)
Weather slide sets and/or filmstrips on clouds and weather awareness and survival (Educational Images Ltd., Order Dept., Box 3456, West Side Station, Elmira, NY 14905)

RADIO AND TELEVISION PROGRAMS

"And now a message from the National Weather Service . . ."—You can bring up-to-the-minute weather information into your classroom or nature center with weather reports from *NOAA Weather Radio*. These reports are transmitted continuously over a special FM frequency. They are specific to the area from which they're being broadcast and include instrument readings from local weather stations, general weather movements in the area, and forecasts and outlooks. The broadcasts are updated every one to three hours (more often if conditions are changing quickly). In severe weather, a special warning system interrupts regular reports. Contact your local Weather Service office for frequencies in your area. You can also get a state-by-state listing of radio frequencies by writing to: National Weather Service Headquarters, Attn: W/OM11, 1325 East-West Highway, Silver Spring, MD 20910. You'll need a special receiver to tune into *NOAA Weather Radio;* they are available at most appliance and general merchandise stores.
The Weather Channel offers 24-hour weather coverage, including local, national, and international forecasts, and many special programs. These include "Weather Classroom," a 10-minute program that can be taped for classroom use; TWC offers a textbook to complement the program with activities, meteorology basics, and reproducible weather charts. TWC offers free cable access to many classrooms as well. For program schedules, see the TWC Web site at http://www.weather.com

SOFTWARE AND ONLINE RESOURCES

Weather: Air in Action (Intermediate and Advanced)—CD-ROM with teacher's lesson plans and activities. Short and long video segments, experiments, facts, maps, and explanation of concepts such as evaporation; discusses solar energy, air masses, the water cycle, the earth's rotation as it affects weather, and more. Glossary, index, and test questions (CLEARVUE/eav, 6465 N. Avondale Ave., Chicago, IL 60631)
The Weather Channel Web site (http://www.weather.com) offers online activities and products, including:

• *Local weather reports*—Online view of local radar for your city, updated every half-hour, and 5-day forecast; satellite image of your region; and weather glossary.

• *Everything Weather* (Advanced)—CD-ROM with information, videos, animation and data; storm analysis; city climate data; interactive activities to track hurricanes, name clouds, and calculate wind chill; glossary; online access to forecasts, and more.

• *Teaching tools,* weather stations, clouds charts, videos in educational editions, maps, online links to education resources, names of regional weather education consultants, and more.

Weather in Action (Intermediate and Advanced)—Part of NGS Kids Network, that offers classroom activities and connects classes to other students and weather experts. Investigates local weather events with observation stations, and includes software, teacher's guide, student handbooks, network connection time, and more (National Geographic Society, Educational Services, P.O. Box 98018, Washington, DC 20090-8018).
Weather-related CD-ROMs (Karol Media, 350 N. Pennsylvania Ave., P.O. Box 7600, Wilkes-Barre, PA 18773-7600)

OTHER ACTIVITY SOURCES

American Meteorological Society offers Project ATMOSPHERE educational materials (Advanced), including slides, books, overhead transparencies, videos, and temperature strips, and teacher training in DataStreme online weather information (AMS, 1200 New York Ave., NW, Suite 410, Washington, DC 20005).
For Spacious Skies—National program seeking to increase awareness and appreciation of the sky through interdisciplinary activities. Offers activity guide and 18" x 24" laminated cloud chart (For Spacious Skies, 54 Webb St., Lexington, MA 02173).
A Guide to Weather Watching by Marty Silver—Part of a series of inexpensive nature study guides (Nature Study Booklets, Warriors Path State Park, P.O. Box 5026, Kingsport, TN 37663).
How the Weatherworks offers videos, flash cards, charts and other materials (How the Weatherworks, 1522 Baylor Ave., Rockville, MD 20850). These include:

- *Weather Study Under a Newspaper & Television Umbrella*—Interdisciplinary study guide focusing on activities to use with newspaper and TV weather reports, articles, and maps.
- *The Cloud Charts*—Three posters on clouds and weather phenomena.
- *The Amateur Meteorologist* by H. Michael Mogil and Barbara G. Levine (Advanced), an interdisciplinary curriculum guide (1993).

OBIS (Outdoor Biology Instructional Strategies)—Offers weather-related activities including "Cool It" and " "Terrestrial Hi-Lo Hunt." The same address offers a Water Cycle Model with 10 study cards (Delta Education, P.O. Box 3000, Nashua, NH 03061).

Project Earth Science: Meteorology (Advanced)—Activities, supplemental readings for educators, and a resource guide (National Science Teachers Association, 1840 Wilson Blvd., Arlington, VA 22201-3000).

Project WILD has conservation education activities with weather units including "Stormy Weather" and "Rainfall in the Forest" (Project WILD, Western Regional Environmental Education Council, 5430 Grosvenor Lake, Bethesda, MD 20814).

Sky Awareness Week every April is a national event dedicated to encouraging everyone to learn about meteorology and astronomy. For a guide to "101 Ways to Celebrate Sky Awareness Week," write How the Weatherworks, 1522 Baylor Ave., Rockville, MD 20850.

Why Does It Rain?—A Wonders of Learning Kit containing 30 student booklets, read-along cassette, and teacher's guide with activity sheets (National Geographic Society, Educational Services, P.O. Box 98019, Washington, DC 20090-8019).

WEATHER SUPPLIES

The WeatherCycler (Intermediate and Advanced)—Slide-chart weather model that explains how you can forecast weather patterns by looking at the interactions of high and low pressure systems. You can use *The WeatherCycler* along with current newspaper and TV weather maps to come up with a forecast. An information booklet on how to use the model is included. A teacher's version, for use with an overhead projector and a set of six student activity sheets, is also available. Developed by Dr. Ira W. Geer (The Weather School, 5805 Tudor Lane, Rockville, MD 20852).

WEATHER INSTRUMENTS

For catalogs and price lists of weather instruments, contact:

- Carolina Biological Supply Company, 2700 York Rd., Burlington, NC 27215. Also offers models, pictures, cloud charts, books, videos and slides.
- Nasco, 901 Janesville Ave., Fort Atkinson, WI 53538-0901 or 1524 Princeton Ave., Modesto, CA 95352.
- National Geographic Society, Educational Services, P.O. Box 98175, Washington, DC 20090-8175; several items include a children's weather station set.

WHERE TO GET MORE INFORMATION

- airports (contact airports in your area to see if school groups can visit their weather stations)
- local TV forecasters
- nature centers in your area
- university departments of meteorology

Internet Address Disclaimer

The Internet information provided here was correct, to the best of our knowledge, at the time of publication. It is important to remember, however, the dynamic nature of the Internet. Resources that are free and publicly available one day may require a fee or restrict access the next, and the location of items may change as menus and homepages are reorganized.

Natural Resources

Ranger Rick, *published by the National Wildlife Federation, is a monthly nature magazine for elementary-age children.*

Ranger Rick magazine is an excellent source of additional information and activities on dinosaurs and many other aspects of nature, outdoor adventure, and the environment. This 48-page award-winning monthly publication of the National Wildlife Federation is packed with the highest-quality color photos, illustrations, and both fiction and nonfiction articles. All factual information in *Ranger Rick* has been checked for accuracy by experts in the field. The articles, games, puzzles, photo-stories, crafts, and other features inform as well as entertain and can easily be adapted for classroom use. To order or for more information, call 1-800-588-1650.

The EarthSavers Club provides an excellent opportunity for you and your students to join thousands of others across the country in helping to improve our environment. Sponsored by Target Stores and the National Wildlife Federation, this program provides children aged 6 to 14 and their adult leaders with free copies of the award-winning *EarthSavers* newspaper and *Activity Guide* four times during the school year, along with a leader's handbook, EarthSavers Club certificate, and membership cards. For more information on how to join, call 1-703-790-4535 or write to EarthSavers; National Wildlife Federation; 8925 Leesburg Pike; Vienna, VA 22184.

ANSWERS TO COPYCAT PAGES:

DRIPPY TALES   (p. 14)

LIGHTNING ON THE LOOSE (p. 35)

WEATHER WISE RIDDLES   (p. 34)

Answers

2. wind 3. snowflakes 4. glaze 5. lightning 6. hail 7. thunder 8. hurricane
9. tornado 10. blizzard 11. fog

MAKE YOUR OWN BAROMETER   (p. 66)

Answer

You will probably find that the weather was cloudy and unsettled, with rain, drizzle, or fog.

CALCULATE A RAINDROP'S SIZE   (p. 67)

Answer

Depending on wind direction and how the container was held, the shapes should vary from nearly circular to elliptical for larger drops.

THE WIND CHILL FACTOR   (p. 69)

Answers

1. Yes, over the indicated time period.
2. Yes, at minute three and at minute eight.
3. For this data and subsequent graph, there was no steady plateau.
4. Depending on how hot the temperature of the water initially was, the thermometer would indicate just the cooling of the water. After reaching room temperature, the evaporation/wind chill curve would be observed.
5. As you climb out of the pool, dry air and light winds "strip away" water molecules from your skin. Each of these molecules also takes with them a "piece" of heat that your body generated. Evaporation is a cooling process and your brain registers your skin being colder.

DETERMINING DEW POINT   (p. 71)

Answers

1. It takes time for the air to become saturated. When condensation formed, the air inside the beaker and above the ice was saturated with water vapor.
2. Yes, after the glass exterior "fogged up."

THE COLD FRONT   (p. 73)

Answers

1. Depending on the size of the tank, condensation formed above the sand bags to near the top of the aquarium.
2. Just below the condensation line.

SATELLITE NEWSPAPER PICTURES   (p. 75)

Answers

1. The answer will depend on the location and the season.
2. In the Northern Hemisphere, they travel from west to east.
3. Yes, the prediction will be made much more accurately if regional readings of temperature, pressure, humidity, and cloud type are used with the satellite photographs.